THE SALT FAT ACID HEAT COOKBOOK

The Ultimate Salt Fat Acid Heat Cookbook for Culinary Mastery and Irresistible Flavors

Dr. Vince Arnold

The information in this book is intended for educational purposes only and is not intended to diagnose, treat, or cure any disease. Readers are advised to consult with their healthcare provider before making any significant changes to their diet or exercise routine.

While every effort has been made to ensure the accuracy of the information contained in this book, the author and publisher assume no responsibility for errors or omissions, or for any consequences resulting from the use of the information contained herein.

Table of Contents

Introduction

In a world filled with countless cookbooks promising culinary mastery and irresistible flavors, there is one remarkable book that stands apart, poised to transform your cooking forever. Welcome to the extraordinary journey of the "Salt Fat Acid Heat Cookbook: The Ultimate Salt Fat Acid Heat Cookbook for Culinary Mastery and Irresistible Flavors." Prepare to unlock the secret code that has captivated chefs and home cooks alike for centuries – the enchanting quartet of salt, fat, acid, and heat.

Picture this: a kitchen filled with the tantalizing aromas of sizzling ingredients, the siren call of crackling fat, and the dance of flavors that harmoniously blend on your palate. Imagine achieving culinary greatness, not through elusive recipes or complex techniques, but by mastering the fundamental building blocks of taste. It's time to liberate yourself from the confines of mediocre meals and embark on a journey towards extraordinary gastronomic experiences.

But let us not rush into the realms of flavor revelation just yet. Instead, allow me to transport you to a bustling marketplace, where ancient culinary secrets are whispered from one generation to the next, and where the quest for culinary perfection has been an eternal flame. Close your eyes and breathe in the vibrant spices of the East, the fragrant herbs of the Mediterranean, and the smoky intensity of Latin American barbecue. Can you feel the anticipation building?

Salt, with its ability to enhance and elevate flavors, takes center stage. Feel the gentle crunch of sea salt as it effortlessly transforms a simple tomato into a burst of umami brilliance. Then, let your mind wander to the tantalizing richness of fat, where butter, olive oil, and rendered drippings create a symphony of velvety textures and indulgent tastes. As your taste buds tingle, journey into the world of acid, where citrus zests and vinegars bring brightness and balance to every dish, awakening the senses like a gust of fresh air. Finally, feel the exhilarating heat that enlivens your senses, from the fiery spice of chili peppers to the controlled intensity of searing flames.

Now, as you open your eyes, allow yourself to imagine the possibilities that lie before you. With the "Salt Fat Acid Heat Cookbook," you hold the key to unlocking the true potential of your culinary creations. Through its meticulously crafted pages, you will be guided through a world where flavor reigns supreme, where the seemingly ordinary is transformed into the extraordinary.

But this cookbook is not merely a collection of recipes; it is a passport to culinary exploration. It is a comprehensive guide that will empower you to understand the intricate relationship between salt, fat, acid, and heat, and how to wield them with precision and finesse. From mastering basic seasoning techniques to delving into the rich tapestry of global flavors, this book will ignite your creativity and embolden you to experiment fearlessly in the kitchen.

So, dear reader, are you ready to embark on this extraordinary journey? Are you prepared to unleash your inner culinary genius and forever change the way you approach cooking? The "Salt Fat Acid Heat Cookbook" beckons you to embrace the power of these four elemental forces and create irresistible flavors that will leave your loved ones in awe.

Come, let us venture forth into a world of culinary mastery, where the alchemy of salt, fat, acid, and heat awaits. Together, we shall turn humble ingredients into culinary triumphs, and ordinary meals into extraordinary feasts. Open your heart, open your mind, and let the magic of the "Salt Fat Acid Heat Cookbook" guide you towards culinary greatness.

"Unleash your Culinary Genius and let The Salt Fat Acid Heat Cookbook be the Catalyst for Your Culinary Triumphs.".

Part I: Salt

Chapter 1: Understanding the Essence of Salt

The Role of Salt in Flavor Enhancement

Salt, a seemingly simple mineral, possesses a remarkable power to elevate the flavors of food and awaken our taste buds. It is the unsung hero of the culinary world, playing a vital role in enhancing and balancing flavors in dishes across cultures and cuisines. Understanding the profound impact of salt on our palates is the first step towards unlocking the true potential of our culinary creations.

At its core, salt is a flavor enhancer. It has the unique ability to magnify the natural tastes and aromas of ingredients, amplifying their inherent qualities and making them more pronounced. When used judiciously, salt can elevate a dish from mere sustenance to a symphony of flavors that dance harmoniously on the tongue.

One of salt's fundamental roles is to bring out the savory quality in food, known as umami. This fifth taste, alongside sweet, sour, bitter, and salty, adds depth and complexity to our culinary experiences. Salt acts as a catalyst, stimulating the taste receptors on our tongues and intensifying the perception of umami in savory ingredients like meats, vegetables, and even dairy products. It helps balance out the other taste components, allowing the full spectrum of flavors to shine through.

Beyond its ability to enhance taste, salt also plays a crucial role in food preservation. For centuries, salt has been utilized as a natural preservative, inhibiting the growth of bacteria and other microorganisms that can cause food spoilage. By drawing out moisture from ingredients, salt creates an inhospitable environment for bacteria, effectively extending the shelf life of perishable foods. The preservation properties of salt have been employed in techniques such as salting, curing, and brining, allowing us to enjoy delicacies like cured meats, pickles, and aged cheeses.

Moreover, salt contributes to the texture and structure of food. It helps in the denaturation of proteins, aiding in the tenderization of meat and fish. In baking, salt controls yeast activity, strengthens gluten development, and adds a touch of complexity to the overall flavor profile of breads and pastries. It is a versatile ingredient that works behind the scenes, subtly influencing the physical properties of our culinary creations.

However, it is important to note that salt's impact on flavor is a delicate balance. Too little salt can result in blandness, dulling the taste of ingredients and leaving a dish lackluster. Conversely, excessive salt can overpower other flavors, leaving a dish overly salty and unpleasant. The key lies in achieving the perfect balance, where salt enhances the flavors without overwhelming them.

As you embark on your culinary journey, remember that salt is not merely a seasoning but a masterful tool in your hands. It is the conductor that brings harmony to the symphony of flavors. With a deep understanding of the role of salt in flavor enhancement, you hold the key to creating culinary delights that will tantalize the taste buds and leave a lasting impression.

So, embrace the power of salt, experiment with different types and applications, and learn to wield its influence with finesse. Allow salt to be your trusted ally as you embark on a flavor-filled adventure, where every dish is transformed into a masterpiece, and every bite becomes an experience worth savoring.

7 Different Types of Salt and Their Applications

Salt, an essential ingredient in our culinary endeavors, comes in a variety of forms, each with its own unique characteristics and applications. From the delicate flakes of sea salt to the robust crystals of rock salt, understanding the different types of salt allows us to explore diverse flavor profiles and elevate our dishes in extraordinary ways. Let's delve into the world of salt and discover the nuances of its various varieties.

1. Table Salt: Table salt, also known as refined salt, is the most commonly used salt in households and commercial kitchens. It is highly refined, often with additives to prevent clumping. Table salt has fine granules and a strong, concentrated flavor. It is ideal for general cooking, baking, and seasoning during or after cooking.

2. Sea Salt: Sea salt is harvested from evaporated seawater. It retains natural minerals and impurities, giving it a slightly briny taste and a range of textures, from fine to coarse. The texture and flavor can vary depending on the source and method of harvesting. Sea salt is versatile and works well in both savory and sweet dishes, adding a subtle complexity to salads, roasted vegetables, grilled meats, and even chocolate desserts.

3. Kosher Salt: Kosher salt, traditionally used in Jewish cooking, is named for its use in the koshering process of meat. It has larger, coarser grains compared to table salt. Kosher salt is prized for its ability to adhere to surfaces, making it ideal for seasoning meats before cooking. Its texture also makes it easy to pinch and sprinkle, providing better control over the amount of salt used. Kosher salt is favored by many chefs for its versatility and its ability to enhance flavors without overpowering.

4. Himalayan Pink Salt: Himalayan pink salt is mined from the ancient salt deposits in the Himalayan mountains. It gets its distinctive pink color from trace minerals present in the salt, such as iron oxide. Himalayan salt is known for its mild, subtle flavor and its unique visual appeal. It can be used in a wide range of applications, including seasoning meats, rimming cocktail glasses, and adding a touch of elegance to various dishes.

5. Flake Salt: Flake salt, characterized by its delicate, pyramid-shaped crystals, is formed by evaporating seawater. It has a light, crunchy texture and a mild flavor. Flake salt dissolves quickly and evenly, making it ideal for finishing dishes, such as salads, roasted vegetables, or grilled fish. Its attractive appearance and delicate crunch add a visual and textural element to culinary creations.

6. Rock Salt: Rock salt, or halite, is a coarse salt typically used in food preservation, brining, and salt crust cooking. It has large, irregular crystals and is commonly found in large chunks or blocks. Rock salt is also used in ice cream makers to create a lower temperature for freezing. While it is not typically used as a table salt, it serves important functions in specific culinary techniques.

7. Specialty Salts: Beyond the commonly used salts, there is a wide range of specialty salts available, each offering distinct flavors and textures. These include black salt (kala namak), which has a sulfurous taste and is used in Indian cuisine; smoked salt, which adds a rich, smoky flavor to dishes; and flavored salts infused with herbs, spices, or citrus zest, providing an instant boost of flavor to various dishes.

When choosing the right salt for a specific dish, consider the texture, flavor, and intended application. Experimentation with different types of salt can enhance the complexity of flavors in your cooking, adding a nuanced touch that elevates your culinary creations to new heights.

So, explore the world of salt, savor its subtle differences, and let it be your companion in your culinary

Finding the Right Balance: Salt in Cooking

Salt, with its remarkable ability to enhance flavors, is a fundamental component of cooking. It has the power to elevate a dish from ordinary to extraordinary, but finding the right balance is key. Understanding how to wield salt with precision and finesse is an essential skill that separates a good cook from a great one. Let's explore the art of finding the right balance of salt in cooking.

1. Enhancing Flavor: Salt acts as a flavor enhancer, bringing out the natural tastes and aromas of ingredients. However, it is important to note that its role is not to overpower the flavors but to harmonize and balance them. Start by using salt sparingly and gradually build up as needed, tasting and adjusting along the way. This allows you to maintain control and ensure that the salt enhances the existing flavors without dominating the dish.

2. Seasoning Throughout the Cooking Process: Salt should be added in layers throughout the cooking process rather than at the end. By seasoning at various stages, you give the salt time to dissolve and infuse into the ingredients, resulting in a more evenly seasoned dish. For example, when sautéing onions, adding a pinch of salt at the beginning helps draw out moisture and develop their sweetness. Similarly, when boiling pasta or blanching vegetables, seasoning the water with salt imparts flavor directly into the food.

3. Taste, Adjust, Repeat: Tasting is a crucial step in finding the right balance of salt. Regularly sample your dish as you cook, making small adjustments as needed. Remember that different ingredients and cooking methods require varying amounts of salt. Taste for saltiness, but also consider how it affects the overall flavor profile—whether it enhances the sweetness, reduces bitterness, or adds depth to the dish. Developing a sensitive palate takes practice, but over time, you'll become more attuned to the perfect balance.

4. Mindful Consideration of Salt in Recipes: When following recipes, it is important to approach the suggested amount of salt as a guideline rather than an absolute rule. Factors such as personal preference, ingredient variations, and dietary restrictions may require adjustments. Understand the overall flavor profile of the dish you're preparing and use the recipe as a starting point. Trust your taste buds and make adjustments accordingly to achieve your desired balance of flavors.

5. Pairing Salt with Other Seasonings: Salt works synergistically with other seasonings to create a harmonious balance of flavors. Consider the other herbs, spices, and ingredients you're using in a dish and how they interact with salt. For example, acidic ingredients like lemon juice or vinegar can enhance the perception of saltiness, while sweet ingredients may require a touch more salt to balance their flavors. Understanding the interplay between salt and other seasonings allows you to create a well-rounded taste experience.

6. Considering Dietary Restrictions: While salt is an important element in cooking, it is essential to be mindful of dietary restrictions, such as low-sodium diets or specific health conditions. In such cases, there are alternative options available, such as using salt substitutes or exploring the natural flavors of herbs, spices, and other seasonings to enhance dishes without relying heavily on salt. Experiment with different flavor profiles and techniques to create delicious meals tailored to individual needs.

Finding the right balance of salt in cooking is a skill that develops with experience, practice, and a keen awareness of your own taste preferences. It requires a thoughtful and mindful approach, respecting the ingredients and allowing their natural flavors to shine. So, embrace the art of seasoning, trust your palate, and let the magic of salt enhance your culinary creations with just the right touch of flavor.

Chapter 2: Salt: The Fundamental Element in Recipes

Mastering Basic Seasoning Techniques

Seasoning is the art of adding the right balance of flavors to your dishes, transforming ordinary ingredients into extraordinary culinary creations. By mastering basic seasoning techniques, you can elevate your cooking to new heights, creating harmonious flavor profiles that tantalize the taste buds. Let's delve into the world of seasoning and explore some fundamental techniques to help you become a seasoning maestro.

1. Salt: As the cornerstone of seasoning, salt enhances flavors and brings out the best in ingredients. Practice using salt judiciously, starting with a small amount and gradually adjusting to achieve the desired balance. Sprinkle salt evenly over ingredients from a height to distribute it evenly. Remember, salt is best added in layers throughout the cooking process, allowing it to dissolve and infuse into the food gradually.

2. Pepper: Ground black pepper adds depth and a subtle kick to dishes. Invest in a good-quality pepper grinder and use freshly ground pepper whenever possible for maximum flavor. Add pepper towards the end of cooking to preserve its pungency, as prolonged cooking can diminish its potency.

3. Herbs: Fresh or dried herbs are a fantastic way to infuse dishes with vibrant flavors. When using fresh herbs, chop them just before adding them to your recipe to preserve their essential oils. For dried herbs, crush them between your fingers to release their aroma. Add herbs early in the cooking process to allow their flavors to meld with the dish. Popular herbs include basil, parsley, thyme, rosemary, and cilantro, among others.

4. Spices: Spices are the soul of many cuisines, imparting rich and complex flavors. Experiment with a variety of spices such as cumin, coriander, paprika, cinnamon, turmeric, and ginger. Toasting whole spices before grinding them can intensify their flavors. Add spices at the beginning of cooking to allow them to bloom and develop their full potential.

5. Acidic Ingredients: Acidic ingredients like lemon juice, vinegar, or citrus zest add brightness and balance to dishes. They can help cut through richness, enhance flavors, and awaken the taste buds. Squeeze fresh lemon or lime juice over finished dishes, or incorporate vinegar into dressings, marinades, and sauces. Remember to add acidic ingredients towards the end of cooking to preserve their freshness.

6. Balancing Sweetness: Sweetness can balance and enhance savory flavors in a dish. Ingredients like honey, maple syrup, brown sugar, or even caramelized onions can add depth and complexity. Use sweeteners sparingly, tasting as you go to prevent overpowering the dish with sweetness.

7. Tasting and Adjusting: Regularly taste your dishes as you cook, especially when seasoning. The key to mastering seasoning techniques lies in developing your palate. Pay attention to the balance of flavors—whether the dish is too salty, needs more acidity, or lacks depth. Make adjustments gradually, adding small amounts of seasonings at a time, until you achieve the desired taste.

8. Building Layers of Flavor: Seasoning is not a one-time affair; it is a gradual process of building layers of flavor. Start with a foundation of salt, then layer in herbs, spices, and other seasonings gradually. Taste and adjust between each addition to ensure a harmonious balance. Building layers of flavor adds complexity and depth to your dishes.

9. Experimentation: Don't be afraid to step outside your comfort zone and experiment with different seasonings. Embrace the diverse flavors from various cuisines and explore new combinations. Trust your instincts and let your creativity guide you in creating unique flavor profiles that reflect your personal style.

Remember, mastering basic seasoning techniques is a journey that requires practice, experimentation, and an open mind. Develop your palate, trust your senses, and have confidence in your ability to

Elevating Dishes with Creative Salt Applications

Salt, with its incredible ability to enhance flavors, is not limited to simple seasoning. When used creatively, salt can elevate dishes to new levels of taste and sophistication. By exploring unique salt applications, you can add depth, complexity, and a touch of culinary magic to your creations. Let's dive into the world of creative salt applications and discover how to take your dishes to the next level.

1. Salt Crusts: Salt crusts are a technique that involves encasing ingredients in a layer of salt before cooking. This method not only seasons the food but also helps to retain moisture, resulting in succulent, perfectly cooked dishes. Whole fish, chicken, or vegetables can be encased in a mixture of salt, herbs, and spices, creating a flavorful crust that seals in the juices. The salt crust can be cracked open and discarded before serving, leaving behind beautifully seasoned and tender fare.

2. Infused Salts: Infused salts are a wonderful way to add a burst of flavor to your dishes. Start with a high-quality salt, such as sea salt or kosher salt, and infuse it with various ingredients. The options are endless—think citrus zest, dried herbs, spices, truffle oil, or even dried mushrooms. Simply combine the salt with your chosen flavorings and allow it to sit and infuse for a period of time. The resulting infused salt can be used as a finishing touch to sprinkle over dishes, adding a unique and aromatic flavor.

3. Smoked Salt: Smoked salt adds a delightful smoky flavor to dishes, reminiscent of cooking over an open fire. It is created by smoking salt crystals over aromatic wood chips, infusing them with the rich, smoky essence. Use smoked salt as a finishing touch on grilled meats, roasted vegetables, or even sprinkled over creamy soups or stews. The smoky notes will add complexity and a touch of intrigue to your dishes.

4. Seasoned Salt Blends: Create your own signature seasoned salt blends by combining different herbs, spices, and aromatics with salt. This allows you to customize the flavors to suit your personal preferences. Blend ingredients like garlic powder, onion powder, paprika, dried herbs, chili flakes, or even dried fruits and nuts with salt to create a versatile seasoning blend. Use these blends to season meats, vegetables, or even sprinkle over popcorn for a flavor-packed snack.

5. Salted Caramel: Salted caramel is a divine combination of sweet and salty flavors that can transform desserts, baked goods, and even beverages. The addition of a pinch of salt to caramel adds a savory depth that balances the sweetness and intensifies the overall flavor profile. Drizzle salted caramel over ice cream, incorporate it into cakes or cookies, or even stir it into your morning coffee for a delightful twist.

6. Finishing Salts: Finishing salts are premium salts with unique textures and flavors that are sprinkled over dishes just before serving to add a final touch of taste and visual appeal. Examples include delicate flake salts, pyramid-shaped salts, or colorful mineral-rich salts like pink Himalayan salt or black lava salt. These salts can provide a satisfying crunch, a subtle burst of salinity, and an elegant finishing touch to elevate your plated creations.

7. Salt Rimmed Glasses: Salt-rimmed glasses add a pop of flavor and an enticing visual element to cocktails and beverages. Moisten the rim of a glass with citrus juice or water, then dip it into a plate of flavored salt, such as margarita salt or celery salt. The salt rim not only enhances the taste experience but also complements and balances the flavors of the drink.

When it comes to creative salt applications, the key is experimentation and imagination. Don't be afraid to venture

Exploring Salt-Curing and Brining Techniques

Salt-curing and brining are age-old preservation methods that not only help extend the shelf life of food but also infuse them with incredible flavors and textures. By immersing ingredients in salt or brine solutions, you can transform ordinary ingredients into culinary delights. Let's explore the art of salt-curing and brining and discover how these techniques can enhance your dishes.

1. Salt-Curing: Salt-curing involves using salt to draw out moisture from food, creating an inhospitable environment for bacteria and preserving the ingredient. This process not only preserves the food but also concentrates flavors, adds complexity, and enhances texture. Here are a few examples of salt-curing techniques:

- Dry Salt-Curing: In this method, food items such as fish, meat, or even vegetables are coated with salt and left to cure for a specific period. The salt draws out moisture, preserving the food and intensifying flavors. Dry salt-cured foods like salt-cured fish (e.g., salted cod or gravlax) or salt-cured pork (e.g., prosciutto or bacon) have a rich, concentrated taste that can be enjoyed in a variety of dishes.

- Wet Salt-Curing: Wet salt-curing involves submerging the ingredient in a saltwater brine solution. This method is commonly used for items like olives or pickles, where the brine helps preserve and flavor the food. The saltwater brine infuses the ingredients with a savory taste and enhances their texture.

2. Brining: Brining is the process of soaking food in a solution of salt and water (sometimes with additional seasonings) known as a brine. This technique is primarily used to enhance the flavor, tenderness, and juiciness of meats, poultry, and certain vegetables. Brining works through osmosis, allowing the saltwater solution to penetrate the cells of the food, resulting in seasoned, succulent, and well-seasoned dishes. Here are a few key points about brining:

- Meat and Poultry Brining: Brining meat or poultry before cooking can result in juicy and flavorful dishes. By submerging the protein in a brine solution, the salt and seasonings permeate the meat, enhancing its natural flavor and ensuring it remains moist during cooking. Brining is particularly beneficial for lean cuts of meat, such as turkey breast or chicken breast, which tend to dry out during cooking.

- Vegetable Brining: Brining can also be used for certain vegetables, such as cucumbers in the process of making pickles. The brine solution imparts flavor and helps to preserve the crisp texture of the vegetables. This technique can be adapted to other vegetables as well, allowing you to experiment with different flavors and textures.

3. Flavoring Brines: Brines can be customized by adding various aromatics, herbs, spices, and even sweeteners to infuse additional flavors into the food. Popular additions include bay leaves, peppercorns, garlic, citrus zest, herbs like rosemary or thyme, and even sweeteners like sugar or maple syrup. These additional ingredients complement the natural flavors of the food being brined, creating a complex and aromatic taste profile.

4. Brining Duration and Techniques: The duration of brining depends on the size and type of the food being brined. For example, smaller cuts of meat or poultry may require just a few hours, while larger cuts or whole birds may benefit from overnight brining. It's important to follow recommended brining times to prevent over-seasoning or texture changes.

- Submersion Brining: This method involves fully immersing the food in the brine solution. Use a non-reactive container (e.g., stainless steel or glass) that is large enough to hold the food and the brine solution. Ensure that the food is fully submerged in the brine, and refrigerate during the brining process to maintain food safety.
- Injection Brining: Injection brining is suitable for larger cuts of meat, such as whole turkeys or roasts. Using a brine injector, the brine solution is injected directly into the meat, allowing for deeper penetration of flavors and moisture.

5. Post-Brining Considerations: After the brining process, it's important to rinse the food thoroughly to remove excess salt from the surface. This step prevents the dish from becoming overly salty. Pat the food dry before cooking to ensure proper browning and texture.

6. Cooking Techniques: Salt-cured and brined ingredients can be cooked using various methods, such as grilling, roasting, smoking, or pan-searing. The salt or brine imparts a flavorful foundation to the food, enhancing the overall taste and tenderness. Be mindful of the salt content in your dish when seasoning during the cooking process, as the cured or brined food may require less additional salt.

7. Experimentation and Creativity: Salt-curing and brining offer endless opportunities for experimentation and creativity in the kitchen. Explore different combinations of herbs, spices, and aromatics to create unique flavor profiles. You can also incorporate additional ingredients like citrus, wine, or even aromatics like star anise or cinnamon to infuse exciting flavors.

Remember, salt-curing and brining techniques require attention to detail, precise measurements, and adherence to recommended brining times. With practice, you'll develop a sense of how salt and brine can transform ingredients, resulting in flavorful and moist dishes that are sure to impress. So, dive into the world of salt-curing and brining, and elevate your culinary repertoire to new heights.

Chapter 3: From Simple to Sublime: Salt in Every Cuisine

Salting Techniques in Mediterranean Cuisine

Salt has played a fundamental role in Mediterranean cuisine for centuries, imparting flavors, preserving ingredients, and creating a distinct culinary identity. The diverse cultures of the Mediterranean region have developed various salting techniques that contribute to the vibrant and robust flavors found in their traditional dishes. Let's delve into the salting techniques used in Mediterranean cuisine and discover how they enhance the taste and character of the food.

1. Dry Salting: Dry salting involves coating or rubbing ingredients with salt and allowing them to rest for a period of time. This technique draws out moisture from the food, intensifies flavors, and helps to preserve it. Here are a few examples of dry salting techniques:

- Dry Salted Fish: Salting fish, such as salted cod (bacalao), is a traditional practice in Mediterranean countries like Portugal, Spain, and Italy. The fish is heavily salted and left to dry for a certain period, which removes moisture and concentrates the flavors. This process not only preserves the fish but also imparts a unique savory taste, making it a key ingredient in various Mediterranean dishes.

- Salt-Cured Meats: The Mediterranean region is renowned for its salt-cured meats, such as prosciutto, jamón ibérico, or bresaola. Meats are generously coated with salt and sometimes a blend of herbs and spices, then allowed to cure and dry for an extended period. This process preserves the meat, intensifies its flavor, and creates a characteristic richness that is highly prized in Mediterranean cuisine.

2. Brining and Salting: Brining and salting techniques are commonly used in Mediterranean cuisine to add flavor, tenderness, and succulence to ingredients. Here are a few examples:

- Olives: Olives, a staple of Mediterranean cuisine, are brined or salted to remove their natural bitterness and enhance their flavor. They are soaked in a brine solution or packed in salt to ferment, resulting in a wide range of briny, tangy, or even herb-infused olives that are enjoyed as standalone snacks or used as ingredients in salads, sauces, and other dishes.

- Pickled Vegetables: Various vegetables, such as cucumbers, cauliflower, or eggplant, are pickled using a brine solution infused with salt, vinegar, and spices. This technique preserves the vegetables while adding a delightful tang and complexity to their flavors. Pickled vegetables are commonly enjoyed as antipasti, accompaniments to main dishes, or incorporated into Mediterranean salads.

3. Salt-Baked Dishes: Salt-baking is a unique technique used in Mediterranean cuisine to cook ingredients inside a salt crust, sealing in moisture and infusing them with savory flavors. Here's how it works:

- Salt-Baked Fish: Whole fish, such as sea bass or red snapper, are often prepared by encasing them in a layer of salt mixed with egg whites and water. The salt crust helps to retain moisture, resulting in tender, flavorful fish. Once baked, the salt crust is cracked open, revealing perfectly cooked and seasoned fish.

4. Salt-Preserved Citrus: Preserving citrus fruits in salt is a traditional technique used in Mediterranean cooking to harness their vibrant flavors. Lemons, oranges, or even preserved lemon peels are generously coated in salt and left to ferment for several weeks. The process softens the bitterness of the pith and imbues the fruit with a unique tangy, salty flavor. Preserved citrus is commonly used in tagines, salads, dressings, and marinades to add a distinct Mediterranean twist.

5. Seasoning with Sea Salt: Sea salt, harvested from Mediterranean coastal areas, holds a special place in Mediterranean cuisine. It is used as a finishing touch to enhance flavors and add texture to dishes.

- Fleur de Sel: Fleur de sel, meaning "flower of salt," is a delicate, hand-harvested sea salt with a slightly moist texture. It is often sprinkled over dishes just before serving to provide a burst of salinity and enhance the overall taste experience. Fleur de sel is particularly valued for its nuanced flavor and is commonly used in Mediterranean salads, grilled vegetables, or even desserts like chocolate.

- Maldon Salt: Maldon salt is another popular sea salt that originates from the Mediterranean region. It is known for its pyramid-shaped flakes and distinctive flaky texture. The flakes are sprinkled over dishes, adding a delightful crunch and a touch of saltiness. Maldon salt is frequently used to finish grilled meats, roasted vegetables, or simply to elevate the flavors of fresh tomatoes, mozzarella, and basil in a classic Caprese salad.

6. Salting in Mediterranean Breads and Pastries: Salt plays a crucial role in the preparation of various breads and pastries in Mediterranean cuisine. It enhances the flavor, aids in fermentation, and helps to regulate yeast activity. From traditional Mediterranean breads like focaccia or ciabatta to delectable pastries like puff pastry or baklava, salt is a key ingredient that contributes to the overall taste and texture of these beloved treats.

7. Balancing Salinity in Mediterranean Dishes: In Mediterranean cuisine, achieving the right balance of salt is essential for creating harmonious flavors. The region's culinary traditions often involve combining salty ingredients, such as cured meats, cheeses, or olives, with fresh produce, aromatic herbs, and olive oil to achieve a balanced and satisfying taste profile. Careful consideration of salt levels in each component of a dish helps to ensure that flavors are well-balanced and not overpowering.

Mediterranean cuisine's skillful use of salt encompasses various techniques that have been perfected over generations. Whether it's the dry salting of fish, the brining of olives, or the delicate finishing touch of sea salt, these techniques contribute to the distinctive and beloved flavors of Mediterranean dishes. So, embrace the art of salting in Mediterranean cuisine and embark on a culinary journey filled with vibrant tastes and aromatic delights.

Asian Salting Traditions and Flavor Profiles

Salt is an essential ingredient in Asian cuisine, playing a vital role in enhancing flavors, preserving ingredients, and creating a harmonious balance in dishes. Asian culinary traditions have developed unique salting techniques that contribute to the diverse and rich flavor profiles found in the region's cuisine. Let's explore the salting traditions and flavor profiles of various Asian cuisines and discover how salt transforms their culinary offerings.

1. Soy Sauce and Fish Sauce: In many Asian countries, soy sauce and fish sauce are fundamental elements in cooking and seasoning. These fermented sauces provide a salty umami flavor that enhances the taste of a wide range of dishes. Here are some examples:

- Soy Sauce: Soy sauce, made from fermented soybeans, wheat, and salt, is a staple in Chinese, Japanese, and Korean cuisines. It adds depth, richness, and a savory umami taste to stir-fries, marinades, dipping sauces, and soups. Light soy sauce is saltier and used for seasoning, while dark soy sauce offers a deeper flavor and is often used for color and richness.
- Fish Sauce: Fish sauce, commonly used in Southeast Asian cuisines such as Thai, Vietnamese, and Filipino, is made from fermented fish or shrimp and salt. It provides a distinct salty, savory, and slightly fishy flavor to dishes. Fish sauce is used in marinades, dressings, stir-fries, and curries, adding a

unique depth of flavor that is characteristic of Asian cuisine.

2. Salted Fermented Ingredients:

Asian cuisines have a rich tradition of fermenting ingredients with salt, resulting in unique flavors and textures. Here are a few examples:

- Salted Shrimp Paste: Belacan in Malaysian and Indonesian cuisine, and bagoong in Filipino cuisine, are salted and fermented shrimp pastes. They are intensely salty and pungent, adding depth and complexity to curries, stews, and sauces.
- Salted Soybean Paste: Fermented soybean pastes like miso in Japanese cuisine and doenjang in Korean cuisine are made by fermenting soybeans with salt and other ingredients. They provide a salty, savory, and slightly sweet flavor that is used as a base for soups, marinades, and sauces.
- Salted Vegetables: Salted vegetables are commonly found in Asian cuisine, such as Chinese salted mustard greens or Korean salted cabbage (kimchi). These fermented and salted vegetables offer a tangy,

salty, and umami flavor that complements various dishes, including stir-fries, soups, and rice dishes.

3. Brining and Salting: Asian cuisines also utilize brining and salting techniques to enhance flavors and textures. Here are a few examples:

- Salted Fish and Seafood: Salted fish and seafood are prevalent in Asian cooking. Salted fish, such as salted mackerel or salted cod, are used in Chinese, Thai, and Malaysian cuisine to provide a distinctive saltiness and depth of flavor to stir-fries, soups, and fried rice dishes.
- Salted Duck Eggs: Salted duck eggs are a popular ingredient in Chinese and Filipino cuisines. Duck eggs are cured in a salt solution, resulting in a rich and salty yolk. They are often used in savory dishes like steamed or stir-fried dishes, imparting a unique salted richness.

4. Seasoning Techniques and Salt Substitutes: Asian cuisines incorporate a variety of seasoning techniques to achieve balanced flavors. In some cases, salt is substituted with other ingredients:

- Seaweed: Dried seaweed, such as nori in Japanese cuisine or laver in Korean cuisine, is often used to season dishes. It adds a natural saltiness and umami flavor that enhances the overall taste of soups, rice dishes, and sushi.
- Fermented Bean Paste: Fermented bean pastes like doubanjiang in Sichuan cuisine or tauchu in Malaysian cuisine are made from fermented soybeans and various seasonings. They provide a complex, salty, and savory flavor to stir-fries, braised dishes, and soups.
- Shrimp Paste: Shrimp paste, commonly used in Southeast Asian cuisines, is made from fermented ground shrimp mixed with salt. It adds a distinctive, salty, and briny flavor to curries, stir-fries, and dipping sauces.
- MSG (Monosodium Glutamate): MSG is a flavor enhancer commonly used in Asian cuisines. Although it is not salt itself, it provides a savory taste that enhances the perception of saltiness and umami flavors in dishes.

5. Balancing Flavors in Asian Cuisine: Asian cuisines emphasize achieving a delicate balance of flavors, including saltiness. The saltiness is often balanced with other elements such as sweetness, sourness, and spiciness. Ingredients like sugar, vinegar, citrus juices, and chili peppers are used to harmonize and counterbalance the saltiness, creating a well-rounded and complex flavor profile.

In Asian cuisine, the art of salting encompasses a wide range of techniques and ingredients, each contributing to the unique flavor profiles found in the region's dishes. From the umami richness of soy sauce and fish sauce to the complexity of fermented ingredients and the careful balance of flavors, salt plays a crucial role in elevating Asian cuisine to new heights. So, explore the vibrant world of Asian salting traditions and savor the incredible flavors that result from these time-honored techniques.

Salt in South American and African Culinary Traditions

Salt is an essential ingredient deeply intertwined with the culinary traditions of both South America and Africa. It not only enhances flavors but also plays a crucial role in preserving food and creating a distinct taste profile in traditional dishes. Let's explore how salt is used in the culinary traditions of these regions and the unique flavor profiles it creates.

South American Culinary Traditions:

1. Curing and Preserving: In South America, salt has been used for centuries as a method of preserving meat, particularly in countries like Argentina, Uruguay, and Brazil. Large cuts of beef, such as the famous Argentinean beef, are salted and air-dried to create mouthwatering cured meats like beef jerky or charqui. The salt draws out moisture from the meat, preventing the growth of bacteria and preserving it for longer periods. These salted and cured meats are then enjoyed as snacks or incorporated into traditional dishes like empanadas or stews, providing intense flavors and enhancing the overall taste experience.

2. Seasoning and Marinating: Salt is a fundamental seasoning in South American cuisine, where it is used to enhance the natural flavors of various ingredients. In countries like Peru and Bolivia, ceviche, a popular dish made with fresh seafood marinated in citrus juices, relies on the perfect balance of salt to bring out the flavors of the fish or shellfish. The salt helps to "cook" the seafood, while also imparting a subtle saltiness that complements the tangy citrus juices.

3. Salting and Fermentation: In certain South American countries like Brazil and Colombia, salt is used in the fermentation process to create unique flavors. For example, in Brazil, salted codfish (bacalhau) is a traditional ingredient used in dishes like bolinhos de bacalhau (codfish fritters) or bacalhau à Gomes de Sá (a codfish casserole). The codfish is heavily salted and dried, then rehydrated before cooking, resulting in a distinctive taste and texture.

African Culinary Traditions:

1. Flavoring and Seasoning: Salt is a ubiquitous ingredient in African cuisine, used to season and enhance the flavors of various dishes. In North African countries like Morocco and Tunisia, salt is often combined with aromatic spices like cumin, coriander, and cinnamon to create rich and flavorful spice blends, such as ras el hanout or baharat. These spice blends are used to season stews, tagines, and couscous, infusing the dishes with complex flavors and aromas.

2. Preserving and Fermentation: Salt has long been used in African culinary traditions as a means of preserving food, particularly in regions where refrigeration is limited. In countries like South Africa, Namibia, and Botswana, salt is used in the preservation of biltong, a type of cured and dried meat. Thin strips of beef or game meat are seasoned with salt and spices, then air-dried until they reach a desired texture. The salt acts as a natural preservative, allowing the meat to be stored for extended periods while maintaining its flavors.

3. Salting in Sauces and Condiments: Many African cuisines incorporate salt into various sauces and condiments to add depth and complexity to dishes. For example, in West Africa, ingredients like salted fish or shrimp are used to create flavor-packed condiments such as egusi sauce or groundnut soup. These condiments are often paired with staple foods like fufu or rice, providing a savory and umami-rich taste.

4. Salting and Grilling: In many African countries, particularly in East Africa, salt is used in the grilling and barbecuing of meats. Meats like nyama choma in Kenya or braai in South Africa are often seasoned with salt and spices, then grilled over open flames. The salt helps to enhance the natural flavors of the meat while imparting a delicious smoky and savory taste. The result is tender, juicy, and flavorful grilled meats that are enjoyed as communal meals and are often accompanied by various sauces and side dishes.

5. Salt in Traditional Stews and Soups: Salt is a vital ingredient in the preparation of traditional stews and soups found across South America and Africa. In South America, dishes like feijoada from Brazil or locro from Argentina rely on the proper seasoning of salt to bring out the flavors of the various ingredients, such as beans, meat, and vegetables. Similarly, in African cuisines, hearty stews like jollof rice in West Africa or bobotie in South Africa are seasoned with salt to create a balanced and flavorful dish. The salt helps to marry the different ingredients and spices, resulting in a harmonious and satisfying taste experience.

6. Salting and Fermenting Vegetables: In certain African cultures, salt is used in the preservation and fermentation of vegetables. In countries like Ethiopia and Eritrea, injera, a traditional sourdough flatbread, is made by fermenting a batter of teff flour mixed with water and salt. The salt not only adds flavor but also helps to regulate the fermentation process, resulting in a tangy and slightly sour bread that is a staple in the region's cuisine.

The culinary traditions of South America and Africa demonstrate the diverse and creative uses of salt in enhancing flavors, preserving food, and creating unique taste profiles. Whether it's curing and preserving meats, seasoning and marinating seafood, or incorporating salt into traditional stews and condiments, salt plays a crucial role in the rich and vibrant cuisines of these regions. So, embrace the flavors of South American and African culinary traditions and savor the culinary delights that salt brings to their dishes.

Part II: Fat

Chapter 4: The Wonders of Fat: A Flavor Catalyst

Understanding the Role of Fat in Cooking

Fat is an essential component of cooking that goes beyond adding flavor and richness to dishes. It plays a vital role in various culinary techniques, contributing to texture, mouthfeel, and overall cooking outcomes. Let's delve into the significance of fat in cooking and explore how it transforms ingredients into delectable creations.

1. Flavor Enhancement: Fat is a carrier of flavor, helping to distribute and intensify the taste of ingredients. When heated, fats like butter, oil, or rendered animal fats release aromatic compounds that enhance the overall flavor profile of a dish. From sautéing onions in butter to frying spices in oil, the fats interact with the ingredients, unlocking their flavors and creating a foundation for the dish.

2. Texture and Mouthfeel: Fat contributes to the texture and mouthfeel of dishes, imparting a luxurious and silky quality. In baking, fats such as butter or shortening add tenderness and moisture to cakes, cookies, and pastries. In savory dishes, fats play a crucial role in achieving a velvety smoothness in sauces, creams, and dressings. They also provide a satisfying richness in dishes like risottos, gratins, or creamy soups, enhancing the overall eating experience.

3. Heat Transfer and Cooking Medium: Fats are excellent conductors of heat, making them essential for various cooking techniques. When used as a cooking medium, fats help to transfer heat evenly and efficiently to ingredients, promoting browning and caramelization. Searing meats in hot oil, stir-frying vegetables in a wok, or deep-frying crispy foods are all examples of how fats facilitate the Maillard reaction, resulting in delicious golden crusts and flavorful exterior textures.

4. Emulsification and Binding: Fat plays a critical role in emulsifying and binding ingredients together. In sauces like mayonnaise or hollandaise, fats act as an emulsifying agent, allowing oil and water-based ingredients to combine into a stable and creamy mixture. Similarly, in baking, fats help to bind ingredients together, providing structure and stability to cakes, pastries, and dough.

5. Heat Transfer and Flavor Extraction: When cooking with fat, it acts as a medium for extracting and infusing flavors from herbs, spices, and aromatics. The fat-soluble compounds in ingredients are released and incorporated into the fat, intensifying the flavors. This technique is commonly used in processes such as blooming spices in hot oil before adding them to a dish, or infusing herbs and garlic in melted butter for aromatic sauces or compound butters.

6. Satiation and Flavor Perception: Fat contributes to the feeling of satiety and satisfaction after a meal. It slows down the digestion process, allowing flavors to linger on the palate for a longer duration. Additionally, fat adds richness and depth to dishes, increasing their perceived flavor intensity and making them more satisfying to consume.

Understanding the role of fat in cooking is essential for achieving culinary mastery and creating irresistible flavors.

From enhancing taste and texture to facilitating heat transfer and emulsification, fat is a versatile ingredient that transforms ingredients into culinary delights. So, embrace the art of using fats in your cooking and unlock a world of delicious possibilities.

Choosing the Right Fats for Different Culinary Applications

Selecting the appropriate fats for different culinary applications is crucial in achieving desired flavors, textures, and cooking outcomes. Various fats have unique characteristics that make them suitable for specific cooking techniques. Let's explore the different types of fats and their best uses in the kitchen:

1. Butter: Butter is a versatile and widely used fat in cooking and baking. It adds a rich, creamy flavor and a smooth texture to dishes. Here are some common uses of butter:

- Sautéing and Pan-Frying: Butter is excellent for gentle sautéing and pan-frying over medium heat. It adds flavor to ingredients and imparts a delightful golden color.

- Baking: Butter is a key ingredient in baking, providing flavor, tenderness, and moisture to cakes, cookies, pastries, and pie crusts.
- Finishing: Adding a small pat of butter at the end of cooking can enrich sauces, gravies, and soups, giving them a luxurious finish.

2. Cooking Oils: Cooking oils are derived from plant sources and offer a range of flavors and smoke points. Here are a few commonly used cooking oils:

- Olive Oil: Extra virgin olive oil is best suited for drizzling over salads, finishing dishes, or lightly sautéing ingredients at lower temperatures. Light olive oil or regular olive oil can be used for higher heat cooking, such as stir-frying or roasting.
- Canola Oil: Canola oil has a neutral flavor and a high smoke point, making it suitable for a variety of cooking methods, including frying, baking, and sautéing.
- Vegetable Oil: Vegetable oil is a versatile and neutral-tasting oil with a high smoke point, making

it ideal for frying, deep-frying, and other high-heat cooking techniques.

3. Cooking Sprays: Cooking sprays are convenient and often used for greasing pans and preventing food from sticking. They typically contain a combination of oils, lecithin, and propellants. They are suitable for baking, grilling, and sautéing, providing a thin and even layer of oil with minimal calories.

4. Rendered Animal Fats: Rendered animal fats, such as lard and duck fat, have distinctive flavors and can add richness and depth to dishes. They are excellent for:

- Frying: Lard and duck fat are favored for deep-frying due to their high smoke points and ability to impart unique flavors.
- Roasting: Using rendered animal fats to coat meats and vegetables before roasting can enhance their flavors and create delicious crispy textures.

5. Plant-Based Fats: Plant-based fats, like coconut oil and avocado oil, offer unique flavors and properties that make them suitable for specific applications:

- Coconut Oil: Coconut oil has a distinct tropical flavor and is solid at room temperature. It is commonly used in baking, vegan recipes, and stir-frying at medium heat.
- Avocado Oil: Avocado oil has a high smoke point and a mild flavor. It is suitable for high-heat cooking, including grilling, sautéing, and roasting.

6. Margarine and Shortening: Margarine and shortening are commonly used as substitutes for butter in baking and cooking. They are typically made from vegetable oils and offer a non-dairy alternative. They work well for baking, creating flaky pastries, and providing a rich texture to cookies and cakes.

When choosing fats for different culinary applications, consider factors such as flavor, smoke point, and desired outcome. Experimenting with various fats can lead to exciting flavor combinations and culinary discoveries. So, explore the world of fats and elevate your cooking with the right choices for each culinary endeavor.

Balancing Fat in Recipes: Techniques and Tips

Finding the right balance of fat in recipes is essential for achieving delicious and well-rounded dishes. Fat contributes flavor, texture, and richness, but it's important to use it judiciously to avoid overwhelming or greasy results. Here are some techniques and tips for balancing fat in your recipes:

1. Consider the Cooking Method: Different cooking methods require varying amounts of fat. For example:

- Sautéing and Stir-frying: Use a moderate amount of fat to coat the pan and prevent sticking. Too much fat can result in greasy dishes.
- Baking: Follow the recipe's fat measurements precisely, as excess fat can affect the structure and texture of baked goods.
- Roasting: Lean meats and vegetables may benefit from a small amount of added fat for flavor and browning. However, fatty cuts may render enough fat during cooking, requiring minimal additional fat.

- Grilling: Use minimal fat directly on the grill grates to prevent sticking, and opt for lean cuts of meat to reduce excessive dripping.

2. Choose the Right Fat for the Dish: Different fats have unique flavors and properties. Consider the flavor profile and cooking requirements of your recipe when selecting fats:

- Neutral Flavors: Use neutral-tasting oils or fats, such as vegetable oil or light olive oil, when you want to let the other ingredients shine.
- Distinctive Flavors: Experiment with fats like butter, coconut oil, or rendered animal fats to add depth and enhance specific flavor profiles.

3. Opt for Healthier Fat Options: While fat is an essential part of cooking, choosing healthier options can promote overall well-being. Consider these alternatives:

- Unsaturated Fats: Incorporate oils rich in monounsaturated and polyunsaturated fats, such as olive oil, avocado oil, or canola oil, which offer health benefits.

- Reduce Saturated Fats: Limit the use of solid fats like butter or shortening, as they contain higher amounts of saturated fats. Substitute with healthier alternatives whenever possible.

4. Use Fat as a Flavor Accent: In some cases, fat can be used as a flavor accent rather than the main ingredient:

- Finish with a Drizzle: Add a small amount of high-quality extra virgin olive oil or melted butter as a finishing touch to enrich the flavors of soups, stews, or roasted vegetables.
- Infuse Flavors: Infuse fats with herbs, spices, or aromatics before using them in recipes. This adds subtle flavors without overwhelming the dish.

5. Incorporate Other Texture Enhancers: Balance the richness of fats by incorporating other ingredients that provide texture and contrast:

- Acidic Ingredients: Add a squeeze of lemon juice, a splash of vinegar, or a dollop of yogurt to counterbalance the richness of fats and brighten the flavors.

- Fresh Herbs and Greens: Incorporate fresh herbs, like parsley or cilantro, or vibrant greens, like arugula or watercress, to add a fresh and lively element to dishes.

6. Practice Portion Control: Keep portion sizes in mind, especially when indulging in dishes rich in fat. Enjoy smaller servings of rich foods to savor the flavors without overloading on fat content.

Balancing fat in recipes requires a thoughtful approach to create well-balanced and flavorful dishes. By considering the cooking method, selecting the right fat, opting for healthier options, and incorporating texture-enhancing ingredients, you can achieve harmonious and delicious results. Experiment with different techniques and embrace the art of balancing fat to elevate your culinary creations.

"Ignite Your Passion for Cooking and Unleash Your Inner Culinary Artist with The Salt Fat Acid Heat Cookbook."

Chapter 5: Mastering the Art of Cooking with Fat

Sautéing and Pan-Frying: Achieving the Perfect Golden Crust

Sautéing and pan-frying are popular cooking techniques that can transform ingredients into delicious dishes with a beautiful golden crust. These methods require attention to detail, proper heat control, and the right techniques to achieve the desired texture, color, and flavor. Here's a guide to help you master sautéing and pan-frying and create that perfect golden crust:

1. Select the Right Pan: Choose a pan that has good heat conductivity for even cooking. A heavy-bottomed skillet or sauté pan with a non-stick surface works well. The size of the pan should accommodate the ingredients without overcrowding, allowing them to cook evenly.

2. Preheat the Pan: Preheating the pan is crucial to ensure a proper sear and the development of a golden crust. Place the pan over medium-high to high heat and allow it to heat for a few minutes until it's hot. Add a small amount of oil or fat and let it heat up as well.

3. Prepare the Ingredients: Ensure that the ingredients you're sautéing or pan-frying are dry. Pat them dry with a paper towel before cooking to remove any excess moisture. This helps in achieving a crispier crust.

4. Season the Ingredients: Season the ingredients with salt and pepper or any desired spices before cooking. This enhances the flavors and provides an even distribution of seasoning throughout the dish.

5. Use the Right Cooking Fat: Choose a fat with a high smoke point for sautéing and pan-frying at higher temperatures. Clarified butter, vegetable oil, canola oil, or grapeseed oil are good options. These fats can withstand the heat without burning, allowing you to achieve a golden crust.

6. Add the Ingredients Carefully: Place the ingredients in the preheated pan carefully to avoid overcrowding. Overcrowding can cause the temperature to drop, resulting in steaming rather than achieving a crisp crust. Cook in batches if necessary.

7. Maintain the Right Heat: Adjust the heat as needed during the cooking process to maintain a consistent temperature. This helps in achieving an even browning and prevents burning. If the heat is too high, the crust may brown quickly while the interior remains undercooked. If the heat is too low, the crust may not develop properly.

8. Avoid Constantly Moving the Ingredients: Allow the ingredients to cook undisturbed for a few minutes to develop a crust. Constantly stirring or flipping can prevent the surface from browning properly. Use a spatula or tongs to flip the ingredients once a crust has formed.

9. Monitor Cooking Time: Keep an eye on the cooking time to prevent overcooking. Sautéing and pan-frying are relatively quick cooking methods, so it's important to monitor the doneness of the ingredients. Cooking times may vary depending on the thickness and type of ingredients.

10. Rest Before Serving: After sautéing or pan-frying, allow the ingredients to rest for a few minutes before serving. This allows the juices to redistribute, resulting in tender and flavorful dishes.

By following these techniques, you can achieve the perfect golden crust when sautéing or pan-frying. Whether you're preparing vegetables, meats, or seafood, mastering these methods will elevate your dishes and impress your taste buds. So, get your pan sizzling hot, choose the right fat, and enjoy the culinary delight of a perfectly golden crust.

Deep-Frying: Crispy Delights and Indulgent Treats

Deep-frying is a cooking technique that involves immersing food in hot oil, resulting in irresistibly crispy and golden delights. From French fries to crispy fried chicken, deep-frying offers a unique texture and flavor that is hard to resist. To achieve the perfect deep-fried treats, follow these guidelines:

1. Choose the Right Oil: Selecting the right oil is essential for deep-frying. Oils with high smoke points and neutral flavors are ideal. Some commonly used oils for deep-frying include vegetable oil, peanut oil, canola oil, and sunflower oil. Avoid using oils with low smoke points, such as olive oil or butter, as they can burn at high temperatures.

2. Use a Deep-Fry Thermometer: Maintaining the correct oil temperature is crucial for successful deep-frying. Use a deep-fry thermometer to monitor the oil's temperature and ensure it stays within the recommended range (usually between 350°F and 375°F or 175°C and 190°C). This helps achieve crispy results and prevents the food from becoming overly greasy.

3. Preheat the Oil: Preheating the oil to the desired temperature is important before adding the food. Heat the oil gradually over medium to medium-high heat until it reaches the desired temperature. This allows the food to cook evenly and minimizes oil absorption.

4. Prepare the Food Properly: Properly preparing the food before deep-frying is essential for achieving the best results. Here are some tips:

- Dry the food: Ensure that the food is thoroughly dried to minimize splattering and excess oil absorption. Pat it dry with paper towels to remove any moisture.
- Coat or batter the food: Coating the food in flour, breadcrumbs, or a batter can enhance the texture and

create a crispy exterior. Dip the food in the desired coating, shaking off any excess before placing it into the hot oil.

5. Fry in Batches: Avoid overcrowding the deep-fryer or pan to ensure even cooking and a crispy exterior. Fry the food in small batches, allowing enough space for the oil to circulate and the food to cook evenly. Overcrowding can lower the oil temperature and result in soggy or greasy results.

6. Maintain Oil Temperature: Maintaining the oil temperature throughout the frying process is essential for achieving crispy and evenly cooked food. Be mindful of adjusting the heat as needed to keep the oil at the desired temperature. Monitor the thermometer and make adjustments to the heat accordingly.

7. Drain Excess Oil: Once the food is deep-fried to perfection, remove it from the oil using a slotted spoon or a wire mesh skimmer. Allow the excess oil to drain by placing the fried food on a wire rack or paper towels. This helps remove any excess oil and ensures a lighter, crispier texture.

8. Season Immediately: Season the deep-fried food with salt or any desired seasonings immediately after removing it from the oil. The heat from the food will help the seasonings adhere and enhance the flavors.

9. Serve and Enjoy: Deep-fried treats are best enjoyed immediately after frying while they are still hot and crispy. Serve them as standalone snacks or incorporate them into your favorite recipes for an indulgent and flavorful experience.

Remember to exercise caution when deep-frying. Hot oil can cause burns, so use appropriate equipment and handle the food carefully. With the right techniques and a little practice, you can achieve crispy delights and indulge in the irresistible pleasures of deep-fried treats. So, heat up that oil, get frying, and enjoy the crispy goodness!

The Art of Rendering: Unlocking Flavor with Fats

Rendering is a culinary technique that involves slowly heating fats to extract their flavor and transform them into a versatile cooking ingredient. This process allows you to unlock the rich flavors and unique qualities of fats, enhancing the taste and texture of your dishes. Whether you're rendering animal fats like bacon fat or exploring plant-based options like coconut oil, mastering the art of rendering can elevate your culinary creations. Here's a guide to help you unlock flavor with fats through the art of rendering:

1. Choose the Right Fat: Select a fat that suits your desired flavor profile and cooking needs. Different fats offer distinct tastes and properties. Some popular choices for rendering include bacon fat, duck fat, beef tallow, lard, and chicken schmaltz. Plant-based options like coconut oil, avocado oil, or even vegetable scraps can also be rendered for unique flavors.

2. Preparation: Start by gathering the fat you want to render and ensuring it is clean and free from any unwanted impurities. If using animal fats, remove any unwanted bits or debris. For plant-based options, make sure the ingredients are fresh and clean.

3. Cut or Grind the Fat: To facilitate the rendering process, cut the fat into small, uniform pieces or grind it. This increases the surface area, allowing the fat to melt more efficiently and evenly.

4. Low and Slow Heat: Place the fat in a heavy-bottomed saucepan or skillet and set the heat to low. Slow and gentle heat is essential for rendering fats. Avoid high heat, as it can scorch the fat and lead to undesirable flavors.

5. Melt and Strain: As the fat slowly melts, stir occasionally to ensure even heat distribution. The process can take some time, so be patient. As the fat melts, it will separate into liquid fat and cracklings or solids. Once the fat is fully melted and the solids have turned golden brown and crispy, it's time to strain.

6. Straining the Rendered Fat: Carefully strain the liquid fat through a fine-mesh sieve or cheesecloth into a heatproof container. This will separate any remaining solids from the flavorful liquid fat. Discard the solids or save them as tasty additions to dishes like soups or stews.

7. Storage and Usage: Allow the rendered fat to cool before transferring it to airtight containers. Store it in the refrigerator or freezer to extend its shelf life. Properly rendered fats can last for several months when stored correctly. Use the rendered fat in various cooking applications, such as sautéing, roasting, frying, or as a flavor enhancer in sauces, dressings, or baked goods.

8. Experiment and Explore: The beauty of rendering fats is the opportunity to explore different flavor profiles and experiment with various ingredients. Feel free to combine different fats or add aromatic herbs, spices, or even citrus zest during the rendering process to infuse unique flavors into your rendered fats.

9. Mindful Usage: While rendered fats can add incredible depth and flavor to your dishes, remember that they are still fats and should be used in moderation. Incorporate them as part of a balanced diet and consider their respective smoke points when determining their best usage.

The art of rendering allows you to unlock the true essence and flavor of fats, adding a distinct richness to your cooking. By choosing the right fats, patiently rendering them with low heat, and utilizing the resulting liquid fat in various dishes, you can create culinary masterpieces bursting with flavor. So, embrace the art of rendering and let the world of flavors unfold before you.

Chapter 6: Fat Around the World: Culinary Traditions Explored

French Cuisine: Celebrating Butter and Cream

French cuisine is renowned worldwide for its rich and indulgent flavors, and a significant part of its allure comes from the generous use of butter and cream. Butter and cream are considered essential ingredients in traditional French cooking, adding a luxurious touch to dishes and elevating their taste and texture. Let's explore how butter and cream play a prominent role in French cuisine and contribute to its culinary excellence:

1. Butter: The Golden Elixir

Butter is often referred to as the "golden elixir" of French cuisine, and its importance cannot be overstated. French chefs take great pride in the quality of their butter, valuing its richness and distinctive flavor. The high butterfat content in French butter gives it a creamy and velvety texture that enhances both savory and sweet preparations.

In French cuisine, butter is used in a multitude of ways:

- Sautéing and Pan-frying: Butter provides a rich and flavorful base for cooking meats, fish, and vegetables, infusing them with a distinct buttery taste.
- Sauces: Butter is an integral component of classic French sauces, such as beurre blanc, beurre noisette, and hollandaise, adding richness and a silky smooth texture.
- Baking: Butter is a staple in French pastry, lending flakiness to croissants, richness to cakes, and a buttery crust to tarts and pastries.

2. Cream: Luxurious and Silky

Cream is another star ingredient in French cuisine, known for its luxurious and silky texture. Its richness adds depth and smoothness to dishes, creating a velvety mouthfeel that is synonymous with French gastronomy.

Cream finds its way into various French recipes:

- Soups and Sauces: Cream is used to enrich and thicken soups, such as the famous velouté or vichyssoise. It adds a luxurious touch to sauces, creating a smooth and luscious consistency.
- Desserts: From classic crème brûlée to mousses, tarts, and pastries, cream is a key component in French dessert making. It adds a delightful richness and creates a creamy, melt-in-your-mouth experience.

3. Balancing Act: Moderation and Technique

While butter and cream play integral roles in French cuisine, it is important to note that moderation and proper technique are essential for achieving the desired flavors without overwhelming the palate. French chefs understand the delicate balance between richness and subtlety, using butter and cream judiciously to enhance, not overpower, the natural flavors of the ingredients.

4. Regional Specialties: Butter and Cream Galore

Different regions in France have their own culinary specialties that showcase the beauty of butter and cream. For example:

- Normandy: Known for its rich dairy products, Normandy celebrates the use of butter and cream in dishes like Normandy-style chicken and tarte Tatin.
- Brittany: Famous for its crêpes and galettes, Brittany embraces the creaminess of butter in both sweet and savory preparations.
- Alsace: This region's cuisine features dishes like choucroute garnie, where cream is used to balance the hearty flavors of sauerkraut and cured meats.

In French cuisine, butter and cream are not just ingredients; they are integral components that add depth, richness, and a touch of indulgence to dishes. Their careful and skillful usage elevates the culinary experience and reflects the artistry of French gastronomy. So, embrace the celebration of butter and cream in French cuisine, and savor the sumptuous delights that they bring to the table.

The Richness of Middle Eastern and Indian Cooking

Middle Eastern and Indian cuisines are renowned for their vibrant flavors, aromatic spices, and an abundance of rich and indulgent dishes. These culinary traditions embrace a wide array of ingredients and cooking techniques that create a tapestry of complex and captivating flavors. Let's delve into the richness of Middle Eastern and Indian cooking and discover what makes them so unique and enticing:

1. Flavorful Spices and Aromatics: Both Middle Eastern and Indian cuisines heavily rely on a diverse range of spices and aromatics, which are the foundation of their distinctive flavors. From cumin, coriander, and turmeric to cardamom, cinnamon, and saffron, these spices lend depth, warmth, and complexity to dishes. Aromatics like garlic, ginger, and onions further enhance the flavor profiles, creating a harmonious blend of tastes.

2. Creamy and Fragrant Sauces: Sauces and gravies play a vital role in Middle Eastern and Indian cooking, adding richness and a luscious texture to the dishes. In Middle Eastern cuisine, tahini-based sauces, such as hummus and baba ghanoush, provide a creamy and nutty element. Indian cuisine boasts an array of gravies, such as tomato-based masalas, coconut milk curries, and yogurt-based sauces like raita, which contribute to the indulgent nature of the cuisine.

3. Indulgent Dairy Products: Dairy products hold a special place in both Middle Eastern and Indian cooking, lending their creamy and luxurious textures to various dishes. In Middle Eastern cuisine, labneh (strained yogurt), feta cheese, and rich cream-based desserts like baklava are cherished. Indian cuisine utilizes ingredients like ghee (clarified butter), paneer (Indian cottage cheese), and thickened milk-based sweets like ras malai and kulfi, showcasing the opulence of dairy in the culinary repertoire.

4. Decadent Sweets and Desserts: Middle Eastern and Indian cuisines offer a wide array of sumptuous sweets and desserts that celebrate the richness of flavors. In the Middle East, delicacies like baklava, knafeh, and halva feature layers of nuts, honey, and fragrant syrups. Indian desserts like gulab jamun, jalebi, and kheer are made with condensed milk, ghee, and an assortment of nuts and spices, creating heavenly treats that delight the taste buds.

5. Slow Cooking and Braising: Middle Eastern and Indian cooking often involve slow cooking and braising methods, allowing the flavors to develop and intensify over time. In Middle Eastern cuisine, dishes like slow-cooked lamb shawarma or tender stewed meats in tagines showcase the art of patience and the resulting succulence. Indian cuisine boasts flavorful curries and biryanis, where slow cooking allows the spices to infuse and meld with the ingredients, resulting in deeply satisfying and flavorful dishes.

6. Staple Ingredients: Nuts, Legumes, and Grains: Nuts, legumes, and grains play a significant role in both Middle Eastern and Indian cooking, adding richness and depth to dishes. Ingredients like almonds, pistachios, chickpeas, lentils, basmati rice, and aromatic couscous are integral components that contribute to the heartiness and luxurious nature of the cuisine.

7. Presentation and Garnishes: Middle Eastern and Indian cuisines emphasize the visual appeal of their dishes, often presenting them with an array of vibrant garnishes. Fresh herbs, such as mint, cilantro, and parsley, provide a burst of freshness, while pomegranate seeds, toasted nuts, and edible flowers add texture and visual interest. These garnishes not only enhance the presentation but also contribute to the overall richness and complexity of the flavors.

8. Regional Varieties and Culinary Traditions: Both Middle Eastern and Indian cuisines exhibit a remarkable diversity in regional specialties and culinary traditions. Middle Eastern cuisine encompasses dishes from countries like Lebanon, Morocco, Turkey, and Iran, each with its own unique flavors and cooking techniques. Similarly, Indian cuisine is a tapestry of flavors from various regions, such as North Indian curries, South Indian dosas and sambar, and the coastal flavors of Goa. This diversity adds to the richness and depth of the overall culinary experience.

9. Hospitality and Generosity: Middle Eastern and Indian cultures are renowned for their hospitality and generosity, and this ethos extends to their culinary traditions. The richness of Middle Eastern and Indian cooking is not just about the ingredients and flavors but also about the communal and inclusive nature of sharing meals with loved ones. The abundance of dishes, the sharing of plates, and the warm hospitality all contribute to the richness of the dining experience.

Middle Eastern and Indian cooking captivate the senses with their opulent flavors, aromatic spices, and indulgent ingredients. From the fragrant biryanis to the creamy tahini sauces, these cuisines celebrate richness in all its forms. Whether you're savoring the flavors of a slow-cooked lamb stew or indulging in a decadent sweet treat, Middle Eastern and Indian cuisine will transport you to a world of culinary richness that is sure to leave a lasting impression. So, embrace the richness and embark on a flavorful journey through the vibrant cuisines of the Middle East and India.

Fat in East Asian and Latin American Culinary Styles

In both East Asian and Latin American culinary traditions, fat plays a crucial role in creating rich, flavorful, and satisfying dishes. While the specific types of fats and their uses may vary, the emphasis on utilizing fat to enhance taste and texture is a common thread. Let's explore how fat is incorporated in these two culinary styles, bringing depth and indulgence to the table:

1. East Asian Culinary Styles:

a) Chinese Cuisine: In Chinese cuisine, various types of fats are used to add richness and flavor. For instance, peanut oil, sesame oil, and vegetable oil are commonly employed for stir-frying, deep-frying, and flavoring. These oils lend a distinct nutty aroma and contribute to the characteristic flavor profiles of Chinese dishes. Additionally, rendered animal fats, such as lard and duck fat, are employed sparingly but add exceptional richness and depth to braised dishes and sauces.

b) Japanese Cuisine: In Japanese cuisine, the use of fat is subtle yet purposeful. High-quality oils, such as sesame oil and vegetable oils, are used for sautéing, tempura frying, and dressing dishes like salads. Additionally, fatty ingredients like fatty tuna (toro), marbled beef (Wagyu), and fatty fish like mackerel are celebrated for their luscious texture and umami flavor.

c) Korean Cuisine: Korean cuisine employs a range of fats to achieve bold and savory flavors. Sesame oil, soybean oil, and perilla oil are frequently used for stir-frying, marinades, and seasoning. Gochujang, a popular Korean chili paste, often contains added oil, providing a rich and spicy element to various dishes. Rendered pork fat (ssalddu) is used sparingly to add depth and flavor to stews and soups.

2. Latin American Culinary Styles:

a) Mexican Cuisine: In Mexican cuisine, various fats contribute to the richness and complexity of flavors. Lard, derived from pork fat, has been a traditional staple and is used in dishes such as tamales, refried beans, and traditional tortillas. Additionally, vegetable oils like corn, avocado, and peanut oil are widely used for frying, sautéing, and making salsas and dressings, adding depth and flavor to dishes.

b) Brazilian Cuisine: Brazilian cuisine showcases the use of fats to enhance flavors and textures. One notable example is the use of rendered animal fat called "banha" or "sebo" in the preparation of feijoada, a traditional Brazilian black bean stew. It adds richness and depth to the dish. Additionally, palm oil, known as "dendê oil,' is a distinctive ingredient in Bahian cuisine, providing a vibrant red color and a unique flavor to dishes like moqueca (a seafood stew) and acarajé (a deep-fried dumpling).

c) Peruvian Cuisine: Peruvian cuisine showcases the influence of various cultures, and fats are integral to its culinary style. In dishes like ceviche, marinated fish is often dressed with a mixture of olive oil and citrus juice, providing a balance of richness and acidity. Additionally, the use of ají amarillo, a Peruvian yellow chili, often involves cooking it in oil to release its flavors and create a fragrant and spicy oil infusion.

In both East Asian and Latin American culinary styles, fat is embraced as an essential element that contributes to the overall sensory experience of a dish. Whether it's the nutty aroma of sesame oil in a stir-fry or the indulgent richness of lard in traditional tamales, fat adds depth, flavor, and a satisfying mouthfeel to these cuisines.

Part III: Acid

Chapter 7: Embracing the Tang: The Magic of Acid

Understanding Acidity and Its Impact on Flavor

Acidity is a fundamental element in the realm of flavors, capable of transforming a dish from dull to vibrant, from ordinary to extraordinary. It is a taste sensation that brings brightness, tanginess, and balance to culinary creations. Let's delve into the concept of acidity and explore its profound impact on flavor:

1. The Nature of Acidity: Acidity is a taste sensation that is perceived on the tongue. It is characterized by a sour or tart flavor, which stimulates the salivary glands and adds a refreshing element to the overall taste experience. Acidity can be found naturally in various foods, such as citrus fruits, vinegar, fermented products, and certain types of dairy.

2. Balancing Act: Creating Harmony in Flavor Profiles:

Acidity plays a crucial role in balancing flavors in a dish. It acts as a counterpoint to other taste components like sweetness, saltiness, and bitterness, helping to create a harmonious and well-rounded flavor profile. Acidity can enhance the perception of other flavors, bringing out their nuances and making them more pronounced.

3. Brightening and Refreshing:n Acidity has the remarkable ability to brighten and refresh the palate. It cuts through richness and heaviness, revitalizing the taste buds and leaving a clean, crisp sensation. A squeeze of lemon juice on grilled fish, a splash of vinegar in a salad dressing, or a dollop of yogurt in a spicy curry can instantly elevate the flavors and add a refreshing touch.

4. Flavor Enhancement and Depth: Acidity can enhance the overall depth and complexity of flavors in a dish. It can amplify the natural flavors of ingredients, bringing out their inherent characteristics. For example, a touch of lemon juice can intensify the sweetness of ripe tomatoes, while a dash of vinegar can heighten the earthiness of roasted vegetables.

Acidity can also add a layer of complexity to dishes, making them more intriguing and memorable.

5. Preserving and Fermentation: Acidity has long been employed as a method of food preservation. The process of fermentation, which involves the conversion of sugars into acids by microorganisms, creates a delightful tanginess and depth of flavor in foods like pickles, sauerkraut, and yogurt. The presence of acidity inhibits the growth of harmful bacteria and prolongs the shelf life of these preserved foods.

6. Versatility in Culinary Applications: Acidity finds its place in various culinary applications across different cuisines. In Mediterranean cooking, a drizzle of balsamic vinegar adds a touch of sweetness and acidity to salads and roasted vegetables. In Asian cuisine, rice vinegar and citrus juices like lime and tamarind are used to balance the flavors of stir-fries, soups, and dipping sauces. In Mexican cuisine, the tangy flavor of lime juice is a common accompaniment to dishes like ceviche and tacos.

7. Artful Pairings: Understanding the art of pairing acidity with other flavors is crucial in creating well-balanced and enticing dishes. Acidity can complement and enhance certain ingredients, while in other cases, it can provide a contrasting flavor note. For example, the bright acidity of tomatoes works harmoniously with the creaminess of mozzarella cheese in a Caprese salad. Similarly, the tartness of lemon juice can balance the richness of butter in a lemon butter sauce for pasta.

Acidity is a powerful tool in the hands of a skilled cook or chef, capable of transforming ordinary ingredients into extraordinary culinary experiences. By understanding the impact of acidity on flavor, one can create dishes that are vibrant, balanced, and full of depth. So, embrace the power of acidity and let it be your secret weapon in the realm of flavor exploration.

Harnessing the Power of Different Acids

Acids are diverse and versatile culinary components that can elevate dishes by adding tanginess, complexity, and balance. From the zing of citrus juices to the depth of vinegars and the unique flavors of fermented acids, understanding and harnessing the power of different acids can take your culinary creations to new heights. Let's explore some of the key acids and how they can be used to enhance flavors:

1. Citrus Acids: Citrus fruits, such as lemons, limes, oranges, and grapefruits, are abundant sources of natural acids. These acids, including citric acid, add bright, zesty flavors to dishes. Citrus juices are widely used to enhance the flavors of both sweet and savory recipes. A squeeze of lemon juice can bring out the freshness of seafood, while lime juice can add a tangy kick to salsas and dressings. The aromatic oils present in the zest of citrus fruits also contribute to the overall flavor profile.

2. Vinegar Acids: Vinegars are made through the fermentation process, where sugars are converted into acids by microorganisms. They come in a variety of types, each with its own distinct flavor profile. Common vinegars include white wine vinegar, red wine vinegar, apple cider vinegar, balsamic vinegar, and rice vinegar. Vinegars offer a wide range of flavors, from mild and tangy to sweet and complex. They can be used in marinades, dressings, sauces, and pickling to add acidity and depth to dishes.

3. Fermented Acids: Fermented foods are rich in organic acids produced by beneficial bacteria during the fermentation process. Examples include kimchi, sauerkraut, yogurt, and kombucha. These acids, such as lactic acid, contribute unique flavors and tanginess to dishes. Fermented acids are particularly popular in Asian cuisines, where they are used to add depth and complexity to dishes like stir-fries, soups, and condiments. They also provide probiotic benefits, promoting a healthy digestive system.

4. Vinegar Substitutes: In recipes where vinegar is not available or desired, there are alternative acid options to consider. For example, lemon or lime juice can often be substituted for vinegar in dressings or marinades. Other acid substitutes include tamarind paste, which adds a tangy and slightly sweet flavor, or yogurt, which provides a mild acidity and creaminess to certain dishes.

5. Acid-Base Balance: Understanding the balance between acidity and other flavors is crucial for achieving well-rounded dishes. Acids can be used to balance sweetness, cut through richness, and add brightness to a dish. Balancing acidity with other taste elements, such as sweetness or saltiness, can create a harmonious flavor profile. Experimenting with different acids and finding the right balance is key to achieving culinary mastery.

6. The Impact of Heat: It's important to note that heat can affect the flavor and potency of acids. While some acids, like citrus juices, are best added towards the end of cooking to preserve their freshness and brightness, others, like vinegars, can withstand heat and be incorporated into cooking processes. Understanding the impact of heat on different acids will help you optimize their flavors in your dishes.

Harnessing the power of different acids allows you to explore a wide range of flavors and create culinary masterpieces. Whether you're using citrus juices to brighten up a salad, vinegar to add depth to a sauce, or fermented acids to elevate the complexity of a dish, the diverse world of acids offers endless possibilities for creating delicious and memorable flavors. So, embrace the acidity and unlock the full potential of your culinary creations.

Balancing Acidity in Your Cooking

Acidity is a powerful flavor component that can transform a dish, adding brightness and depth. However, achieving the right balance of acidity is essential to ensure that it enhances the overall flavor profile without overpowering or overwhelming the other elements. Here are some key considerations for balancing acidity in your cooking:

1. Taste Testing: Taste testing is the key to achieving the perfect balance of acidity. Start by adding a small amount of acid, such as lemon juice or vinegar, to your dish and taste it. Gradually increase the amount until you achieve the desired level of tanginess. Remember that it's easier to add more acidity later if needed, but difficult to reduce it once it's too strong.

2. Consider the Dish: Different dishes have varying levels of acidity that work best with their flavor profiles. For example, a bright and tangy salad may benefit from a higher level of acidity, while a delicate seafood dish may require a more subtle touch. Consider the overall flavor profile and ingredients of the dish to determine the appropriate level of acidity.

3. Complementary Flavors: Balance acidity with other flavors in your dish to create a harmonious taste experience. Sweetness, saltiness, and bitterness can all play a role in balancing acidity. For instance, a squeeze of lemon juice can balance the sweetness of a honey-glazed dish, or a sprinkle of salt can offset the tartness of a vinaigrette. Experiment with different combinations to find the perfect balance.

4. Use Different Acids: Don't limit yourself to a single acid source. Experiment with a variety of acids, such as lemon juice, lime juice, vinegars (e.g., white wine vinegar, rice vinegar, or apple cider vinegar), and even fermented acids like tamarind paste. Each acid brings its unique flavor profile, allowing you to achieve different levels and qualities of acidity in your dishes.

5. Consider Cooking Methods: Different cooking methods can impact the intensity of acidity in your dish. Heat can mellow or enhance acidity, so consider when to add acidic ingredients. For example, adding lemon juice or vinegar at the end of cooking can preserve their freshness and tanginess. However, simmering acidic ingredients can reduce their sharpness and blend them more harmoniously with the other flavors.

6. Balance Over Time: Remember that acidity can evolve and balance out over time. Some dishes, especially those that require marinating or resting, may develop a better balance of flavors as they sit. Allow the flavors to meld together before making final adjustments to the acidity.

7. Practice and Adjust: Balancing acidity is an art that requires practice and adjustments based on personal taste preferences. Take note of the amounts and types of acids used in your recipes and how they impact the final result. With experience, you'll develop a better sense of how different acids interact with different ingredients and how to achieve the perfect balance in your cooking.

Balancing acidity is all about finding the sweet spot that enhances the flavors of your dish without overwhelming them. By considering the dish, complementary flavors, cooking methods, and practicing through experimentation, you'll be able to achieve a well-balanced and delicious outcome. So, embrace the power of acidity and let it bring vibrancy and harmony to your culinary creations.

Chapter 8: Cooking with Acid: Techniques and Applications

Acid as a Marinade or Sauce Component

Acids play a crucial role in marinades and sauces, adding depth, tenderness, and flavor to a wide range of dishes. Whether you're looking to tenderize meat, infuse flavors into ingredients, or create a zesty finishing touch, incorporating acid into your marinades and sauces can take your culinary creations to new heights. Let's explore the benefits and techniques of using acid in these components:

1. Tenderizing and Flavor Infusion: Acids have a tenderizing effect on proteins, making them an excellent choice for marinades. The acid breaks down the muscle fibers, resulting in more tender and succulent meat. Additionally, acids help to infuse flavors into the ingredients, allowing the marinade or sauce to penetrate and enhance the overall taste profile. Common acids used in marinades include citrus juices (such as lemon, lime, or orange), vinegar, wine, and yogurt.

2. Flavor Enhancement: Acids act as flavor enhancers, bringing a bright and tangy element to your marinades and sauces. They can balance and uplift other taste components, adding depth and complexity to the dish. The acidity can cut through richness, add a refreshing touch, and amplify the natural flavors of the ingredients. By experimenting with different acids, you can create a wide range of flavor profiles, from subtle and nuanced to bold and vibrant.

3. Marinating Techniques: When using acid as a marinade component, it's essential to consider the marinating time. The duration of marination will vary depending on the protein and the intensity of the acid used. Delicate proteins, like fish or seafood, require shorter marinating times (usually 15-30 minutes) to avoid over-tenderization. For tougher cuts of meat, like beef or lamb, longer marinating times (2-24 hours) are often needed to achieve optimal tenderness and flavor infusion.

4. Sauce Components: Acid is an essential component in many sauces, providing a necessary tanginess and balance. Whether it's a classic vinaigrette for salads, a citrus-based sauce for seafood, or a rich and tangy barbecue sauce, acids like vinegar, citrus juices, or wine can add a delightful twist to your sauces. They can brighten the flavors, cut through richness, and provide a refreshing contrast. Add the acid gradually, tasting and adjusting as you go, to achieve the desired balance.

5. Acid-Base Balance: Maintaining a balance between acid and other flavors in your marinades and sauces is key. Consider the overall taste profile you're aiming for and adjust the amount of acid accordingly. Balancing acidity with sweetness, saltiness, or other flavors will create a harmonious and well-rounded result. Taste-testing throughout the preparation process allows you to fine-tune the flavors to your liking.

6. Variations and Creativity: Don't be afraid to experiment with different acids and combinations in your marinades and sauces. Each acid brings its unique flavor profile, so have fun exploring the possibilities. For example, try combining citrus juice with a touch of honey for a sweet and tangy marinade, or pair balsamic vinegar with herbs and spices for a rich and complex sauce. Let your creativity guide you in creating tantalizing flavor combinations.

7. Safety Considerations: While acids are excellent marinade and sauce components, it's important to handle them with care. Avoid using excessive amounts of acid, as it can overpower the other flavors and potentially negatively affect the texture of the protein. Also, be mindful of marinating times to prevent over-tenderization, especially with delicate proteins. Lastly, ensure that marinades and sauces containing acid are properly refrigerated to avoid any food safety concerns.

Incorporating acid into your marinades and sauces brings a delightful tang and enhances the overall flavor of your dishes. It adds depth, tenderness, and a refreshing element that can elevate your culinary creations. Whether you're grilling, roasting, or sautéing, acid-infused marinades and sauces can take your dishes from ordinary to extraordinary.

When using acid as a marinade or sauce component, it's important to consider the acidity level and the specific flavors you want to highlight. Citrus juices like lemon, lime, and orange lend a vibrant and citrusy note, perfect for seafood and poultry. Vinegars such as balsamic, red wine, or rice vinegar offer a tangy and complex flavor profile, ideal for marinating meats and creating bold sauces. Other acids, such as yogurt or buttermilk, bring a creamy and tangy element, perfect for tenderizing and adding a subtle tang to various ingredients.

To maximize the flavor infusion and tenderizing effect, allow the ingredients to marinate for the recommended time. This allows the acid to penetrate the protein and infuse it with delicious flavors. However, be cautious not to over-marinate delicate proteins as they can become mushy or overly tender. Adjust the marinating time based on the type of protein and the intensity of the acid used.

When using acid in sauces, such as vinaigrettes, dressings, or finishing sauces, the goal is to balance the flavors and provide a pleasant tanginess. It's important to achieve the right balance between the acidity, sweetness, and other flavor elements. Start by adding a small amount of acid and gradually adjust to your taste preference. Consider complementing flavors like herbs, spices, sweeteners, or even a touch of umami to create a well-rounded sauce.

Creativity and experimentation are key when working with acid in marinades and sauces. Don't be afraid to mix and match different acids, herbs, spices, and other flavor enhancers to create unique and tantalizing combinations. The possibilities are endless, and you'll discover exciting flavor profiles that will surprise and delight your taste buds.

While acids add incredible flavor, it's important to use them in moderation and be mindful of food safety. Avoid using acids that are too strong or excessive in quantity, as they can overpower the other flavors and potentially ruin the texture of the protein. Follow safe food handling practices, refrigerate marinating ingredients properly, and discard any leftover marinades that have come into contact with raw proteins to prevent cross-contamination.

Incorporating acid into your marinades and sauces allows you to unlock a world of flavor possibilities. It adds a bright and tangy element that enhances the taste and texture of your dishes. So, embrace the power of acid, experiment with different combinations, and let your culinary creativity shine as you create marinades and sauces that will elevate your meals to new heights of deliciousness.

Pickling and Fermentation: Preserving with Acid

Pickling and fermentation are age-old techniques used to preserve food by harnessing the power of acid. These methods not only extend the shelf life of ingredients but also create unique and complex flavors that can enhance a wide range of dishes. By immersing ingredients in an acidic environment, whether through pickling or fermentation, you can transform their taste and texture, resulting in tangy, vibrant, and long-lasting culinary delights.

1. Pickling: Pickling involves submerging ingredients in a solution of vinegar, water, salt, and various spices or herbs. The acid in the vinegar acts as a preservative, creating an inhospitable environment for bacteria and other microorganisms. This technique is commonly used for preserving fruits, vegetables, and even proteins like fish or eggs. The acid not only preserves the ingredients but also imparts a tangy and flavorful punch.

2. Fermentation: Fermentation is a natural process that occurs when microorganisms, such as bacteria or yeast, convert sugars into acids or alcohol. In the context of food preservation, fermentation involves creating an environment that encourages beneficial bacteria to thrive and produce lactic acid. This acid not only preserves the food but also imparts a unique, tangy flavor profile. Fermented foods include sauerkraut, kimchi, pickles, kombucha, and yogurt.

3. Flavor Transformations: Both pickling and fermentation dramatically transform the flavor of the ingredients. The acid breaks down complex compounds, creating new tastes and textures. For example, pickling can add a pleasant tanginess to vegetables, fruits, or proteins, enhancing their natural flavors and introducing a refreshing element. Fermentation introduces a depth of flavor through the production of lactic acid, resulting in complex, savory, and sometimes tangy profiles.

4. Creative Combinations: Pickling and fermentation allow for endless creativity in combining ingredients and flavors. You can experiment with different types of vinegar, such as apple cider, white wine, or rice vinegar, to create unique profiles. Spices, herbs, and aromatics like garlic, dill, ginger, or chili peppers can be added to the pickling liquid or fermentation vessel to infuse additional layers of flavor. The combinations are limited only by your imagination.

5. Health Benefits: In addition to their flavor-enhancing qualities, pickling and fermentation offer numerous health benefits. Fermented foods contain beneficial bacteria that support gut health and digestion. They can improve the absorption of nutrients and boost the immune system. Pickled vegetables, on the other hand, retain some of their nutritional value while providing a low-calorie, high-fiber option that adds a burst of flavor to meals.

6. Culinary Applications: Pickled and fermented foods can be used in a variety of culinary applications. Pickled vegetables make excellent toppings for sandwiches, burgers, or salads, adding a crunchy texture and tangy bite. Fermented ingredients, such as kimchi or sauerkraut, can be used to enhance the flavors of stir-fries, rice bowls, or as condiments. They can also be incorporated into dips, sauces, or even baked goods to add a unique and tangy twist.

7. Safety Considerations: While pickling and fermentation offer exciting culinary possibilities, it's crucial to follow proper safety guidelines. Ensure that the ingredients and equipment are clean and sanitized to prevent harmful bacteria growth. Use the correct ratio of acid, salt, and water in pickling solutions, and maintain appropriate fermentation conditions, such as temperature and time, to ensure a safe and successful outcome.

Pickling and fermentation are ancient techniques that continue to be embraced for their ability to preserve food while imparting incredible flavors. By immersing ingredients in an acidic environment, you can create tangy, vibrant

Acid in Baking: Unlocking Flavor and Texture

When it comes to baking, acid serves as a powerful ingredient that goes beyond its role as a flavor enhancer. It plays a crucial role in balancing flavors, activating leavening agents, and creating desirable textures in a wide range of baked goods. Whether you're making cakes, cookies, bread, or pastries, understanding the impact of acid in baking can take your creations to new heights of flavor and texture.

1. Flavor Enhancement: Acid adds a pleasant tanginess and brightness to baked goods, enhancing the overall flavor profile. It acts as a flavor enhancer, cutting through sweetness and adding complexity to the taste. Different acids, such as lemon juice, buttermilk, yogurt, or vinegar, bring their unique flavor profiles, ranging from subtle and citrusy to rich and tangy. By incorporating acid into your baked goods, you can create a harmonious balance of flavors that captivate the palate.

2. Activation of Leavening Agents: Acid plays a critical role in activating leavening agents, such as baking powder and baking soda, which are responsible for creating the desired rise and texture in baked goods. When combined with alkaline ingredients like baking soda, acid triggers a chemical reaction that produces carbon dioxide gas. This gas forms bubbles in the batter or dough, causing it to rise and resulting in a lighter, fluffier texture. The acid ensures that the leavening agents work effectively and contribute to the desired structure of the final product.

3. Tenderizing and Moisture Retention: In certain baked goods, acid acts as a tenderizer, breaking down gluten strands and creating a more tender crumb. It also helps retain moisture, resulting in a moist and tender texture in cakes, quick breads, and muffins. Acids like buttermilk, yogurt, or sour cream are particularly effective in this regard, adding a subtle tang while contributing to the overall tenderness and moisture content of the baked goods.

4. Shelf Life Extension: Acidic ingredients can also contribute to the extended shelf life of certain baked goods. The acidity creates an environment that inhibits the growth of mold and other harmful microorganisms, allowing the baked goods to stay fresh for a longer period. This is particularly evident in recipes like sourdough bread, where the natural fermentation process produces lactic acid, resulting in a longer shelf life and complex flavor profile.

5. Acidic Fruits in Baking: Fruits such as citrus fruits (lemons, oranges), berries, and apples bring natural acidity to baking recipes. Apart from their distinctive flavors, these fruits contain acids like citric acid or malic acid, which contribute to the overall taste and texture of the baked goods. They can be used in the form of zest, juice, or even as purees to add a burst of flavor, moisture, and a hint of tanginess to cakes, pies, tarts, and muffins.

6. Balancing Acidity: While acid brings wonderful flavor and texture to baked goods, it's important to maintain a balance. Too much acid can overpower other flavors and affect the structure of the baked goods. It's crucial to follow recipes and measurements carefully to achieve the desired results. Additionally, consider the interaction between acid and other ingredients in the recipe, such as the type of leavening agent used, to ensure a harmonious balance of flavors and textures.

7. Experimentation and Creativity: Baking offers endless opportunities for experimentation and creativity with acid. You can explore various combinations of acidic ingredients, such as adding a splash of lemon juice to a classic vanilla cake, incorporating buttermilk into biscuits for a tangy kick, or using yogurt in place of milk to enhance the moisture and texture of bread. Don't be afraid to

"Let the Power of Salt, Fat, Acid, and Heat Inspire you to Create Culinary Masterpieces that Leave a Lasting Impression."

Chapter 9: Global Flavors with Acid

Citrus Zest and Juices: Mediterranean and Latin American Cuisine

Citrus zest and juices are essential ingredients in Mediterranean and Latin American cuisine, known for their vibrant flavors and refreshing qualities. The zest, which is the outermost layer of the citrus peel, contains aromatic oils that infuse dishes with intense citrusy notes. The juice, on the other hand, brings a tangy and acidic element that brightens and balances flavors. These citrus components are widely used in both sweet and savory dishes, adding a burst of freshness and complexity to the cuisine.

1. Mediterranean Cuisine: In Mediterranean cooking, citrus zest and juices are prominent flavor enhancers. The zest of lemons, oranges, and limes is commonly used to add a zingy and aromatic touch to dishes. Whether it's sprinkled over salads, drizzled on grilled fish, or incorporated into marinades and dressings, citrus zest lends a bright and invigorating flavor. The juice is also extensively used in sauces, vinaigrettes, and desserts, offering a tangy contrast and balancing richness in dishes like lemon-infused olive oil cake or citrus-based seafood ceviche.

2. Latin American Cuisine: Citrus zest and juices are prevalent in Latin American cuisine, where they are used to create vibrant and zesty flavors. In dishes like ceviche, citrus juices are often used to "cook" the raw fish or seafood, adding a fresh and tangy taste. Lime juice, in particular, is a staple in Latin American cuisine, used in marinades, salsas, guacamole, and as a finishing touch to dishes like tacos and grilled meats. The zest is also utilized in desserts, such as key lime pie or orange-infused flan, to provide a burst of citrus aroma.

3. Versatility and Complementarity: Citrus zest and juices offer versatility and complement a wide range of ingredients and flavors. The bright acidity of citrus can cut through richness, balance sweetness, and enhance the overall taste of dishes. Citrus zest adds depth and complexity to savory dishes like roasted vegetables, braised meats, or pasta dishes. In sweets, it adds a refreshing note to cakes, cookies, and custards. Additionally, citrus zest and juices pair well with herbs like basil, mint, and cilantro, as well as spices like ginger and chili, further enhancing the overall flavor profile of the dish.

4. Tips for Using Citrus Zest and Juices: To extract the zest, use a microplane or a fine grater to remove the outermost colorful layer of the citrus peel. Be careful not to include the bitter white pith beneath. The zest can be added directly to dishes or incorporated into marinades, dressings, or baked goods. To extract the juice, roll the citrus fruit firmly on a countertop to release the juice, then cut and squeeze. Strain the juice to remove any pulp or seeds before using. Adjust the amount of zest and juice according to personal taste preferences and the specific recipe requirements.

5. Utilizing Different Citrus Varieties:

Citrus zest and juices offer an array of flavors depending on the variety of citrus used. Lemons provide a bright and tangy taste, while oranges offer a sweeter, fragrant zest and juice. Limes bring a distinctly tart and acidic flavor, perfect for adding a punch to dishes. Grapefruits can provide a slightly bitter and tangy note, adding complexity to both sweet and savory dishes. Experiment with different citrus varieties to explore their unique flavor profiles and find combinations that suit your culinary preferences.

Citrus zest and juices are prized ingredients in Mediterranean and Latin American cuisine, bringing brightness, aroma, and acidity to a wide range of dishes. Their versatility and ability to uplift flavors make them invaluable components in both traditional

Vinegars and Souring Agents in Asian and Middle Eastern Dishes

Vinegars and souring agents play a vital role in Asian and Middle Eastern cuisines, where the balance of flavors is highly prized. These ingredients bring a delightful tanginess and acidity to dishes, enhancing the overall taste and creating a harmonious flavor profile. From vinegars made from rice, fruits, or grains to fermented pastes and souring agents like tamarind or sumac, these elements add complexity and depth to the culinary traditions of these regions.

1. Rice Vinegar: Rice vinegar is a staple in Asian cuisine, particularly in China, Japan, and Southeast Asian countries.

Made from fermented rice, it offers a mild and slightly sweet flavor with a delicate acidity. It is commonly used in dressings, marinades, stir-fries, and pickles, adding a refreshing tang and balancing other flavors in the dish. In sushi and sushi rice seasoning, rice vinegar is a key ingredient for its distinct taste and ability to enhance the umami flavors.

2. Black Vinegar: Black vinegar, commonly used in Chinese cuisine, has a dark color and a complex, smoky flavor. It is made through a fermentation process involving rice, wheat, millet, or sorghum. Black vinegar has a robust acidity with a hint of sweetness and is often used as a dipping sauce, as a component in braised dishes, or as a dressing for cold appetizers. Its unique flavor profile adds depth and richness to the dishes.

3. Tamarind: Tamarind, a tropical fruit, is widely used as a souring agent in both Asian and Middle Eastern cuisines. It has a tangy and slightly sweet taste with a hint of citrus. Tamarind paste or pulp is commonly added to curries, chutneys, and sauces, providing a distinctive sourness and balancing the flavors of spicy or rich dishes. Tamarind's unique tartness is particularly prominent in dishes like pad Thai, sambar, or tamarind-based soups.

4. Sumac: Sumac, a reddish-purple spice, is a staple in Middle Eastern and Mediterranean cuisines. It is made from dried and ground sumac berries, offering a tangy, lemony flavor. Sumac is used as a souring agent and seasoning in various dishes, such as salads, marinades, kebabs, and dips like hummus or tzatziki. Its bright acidity adds a refreshing and citrusy note, enhancing the overall taste of the dish.

5. Fermented Pastes: Fermented pastes, such as miso in Japanese cuisine or gochujang in Korean cuisine, also contribute to the souring element in Asian dishes. Miso, made from fermented soybeans, provides a complex umami flavor with a subtle tang. It is used in soups, marinades, and glazes, adding depth and complexity to the dish. Gochujang, a fermented chili paste, has a spicy and tangy profile, commonly used in Korean stews, sauces, and marinades.

6. Creative Applications: Vinegars and souring agents offer versatility in Asian and Middle Eastern cuisines, allowing for creative applications in various dishes. They can be used to balance the richness of fatty meats, add brightness to stir-fries, elevate the flavors of noodle soups, or bring a tangy twist to salads and dressings. These ingredients provide an opportunity for exploration and experimentation in the kitchen, allowing you to create unique flavor combinations and tailor the acidity to suit your taste.

7. Balancing Act: When using vinegars and souring agents, it is important to strike a balance between acidity and other flavors in the dish. Start with a small amount and gradually adjust according to personal taste preferences. Remember that different types of vinegar or souring agents have varying intensities, so consider their potency when incorporating them into your recipes. Taste and adjust as necessary to achieve the desired level of sourness without overpowering the other flavors.

Vinegars and souring agents are essential elements in Asian and Middle Eastern cuisines, providing a delightful tanginess that enhances the overall taste and complexity of dishes. Their presence adds a refreshing and balancing note to the culinary traditions of these regions, making them indispensable components in the art of flavor harmony.

Acidic Ingredients in African and Caribbean Culinary Traditions

Acidic ingredients play a crucial role in African and Caribbean culinary traditions, infusing dishes with vibrant flavors and contributing to the overall balance of taste. These regions boast a rich variety of acidic ingredients that are used to enhance flavors, tenderize meats, and create tantalizing marinades and sauces. From citrus fruits to tropical acids and fermented products, the acidic elements in African and Caribbean cuisines add a unique and exciting dimension to the culinary experience.

1. Citrus Fruits: Citrus fruits, such as lemons, limes, and oranges, are widely used in both African and Caribbean cuisines to provide a bright and tangy acidity. The zest and juice of these fruits are incorporated into marinades, dressings, stews, and sauces, adding a refreshing and zesty flavor profile to the dishes. Citrus fruits are particularly prominent in seafood-based recipes, where their acidic properties help to balance the richness of the seafood and enhance the overall taste.

2. Vinegar: Vinegar is a versatile acidic ingredient found in various African and Caribbean dishes. Whether it's distilled white vinegar, cider vinegar, palm vinegar, or sugar cane vinegar, each variety brings its own distinct flavor and complexity to the cuisine. Vinegar is used in marinades, pickles, sauces, and condiments, providing a tangy and sharp taste that cuts through rich and fatty flavors. In Caribbean cuisine, malt vinegar is often used to enhance the flavors of fried fish or chips, creating a delightful contrast.

3. Tropical Acids: African and Caribbean cuisines feature an array of tropical fruits and ingredients that possess natural acids, adding unique flavors and acidity to dishes. Ingredients like sorrel, tamarind, mango, passion fruit, and guava are commonly used to create tangy and refreshing beverages, sauces, chutneys, and marinades. These tropical acids offer a balance of sweetness and acidity, creating a harmonious taste that is characteristic of the region's cuisine.

4. Fermented Products: Fermented products are also prevalent in African and Caribbean culinary traditions, offering a distinct acidic element to the dishes. Fermented ingredients like fermented peppers, fermented fish sauce (such as Haitian or African fish sauce), and fermented vegetables contribute a tangy and complex acidity. These ingredients are often used to season stews, soups, and rice dishes, adding depth and richness to the overall flavor profile.

5. Sour Fruit Juices: In some African and Caribbean cuisines, sour fruit juices are used to introduce acidity to dishes. Examples include baobab juice, hibiscus juice (known as bissap or sorrel), and the juice of sour fruits like sour orange or sour cherry. These juices are employed in marinades, beverages, and sauces, imparting a pleasantly tart and tangy flavor to the culinary creations.

6. Acidic Preservation Techniques: African and Caribbean culinary traditions also employ acidic preservation techniques to extend the shelf life of foods while imparting unique flavors. Ingredients like lime or lemon juice, vinegar, and fermented brines are used in pickling and fermenting various fruits, vegetables, and condiments. These preserved ingredients offer a tangy and slightly acidic taste that can be enjoyed as a condiment or used as an ingredient in other dishes.

7. Balancing Acidity: In African and Caribbean cuisines, achieving a balance of acidity is essential to create harmonious flavors. The acidic ingredients should complement and enhance the other flavors in the dish without overpowering them. It's important to taste and adjust the acidity level gradually, adding small amounts of acidic ingredients and assessing the impact on the overall taste. This way, the acidity can be tailored to suit individual preferences while maintaining the desired balance.

Acidic ingredients are an integral part of the vibrant and diverse culinary traditions of Africa and the Caribbean. They contribute a lively tanginess that elevates dishes, balances flavors, and creates a memorable dining experience. Exploring the acidic components in these cuisines allows for a delightful journey into the world of bold and tantalizing flavors.

"Don't Just Cook; Create Magic in the Kitchen with the Transformative Elements of Salt, Fat, Acid, and Heat at your Fingertips."

Part IV: Heat

Chapter 10: The Transformative Power of Heat

Understanding Different Heat Sources

Heat is a fundamental element in cooking, and understanding the different heat sources available to us allows for precise and effective culinary techniques. Each heat source offers unique characteristics, temperatures, and cooking methods, providing cooks with the flexibility to achieve desired results. Whether it's direct heat, radiant heat, or conductive heat, mastering these heat sources is key to creating delicious and well-cooked dishes.

1. Direct Heat: Direct heat refers to cooking methods where the heat source is in direct contact with the food. This includes grilling, broiling, and pan-frying. Grilling involves placing food on a grate directly above a heat source, such as charcoal or gas flames, allowing for the direct transfer of heat and the development of caramelization and smoky flavors. Broiling, on the other hand, utilizes overhead heat from the oven's broiler element to cook food quickly and create a beautifully browned crust. Pan-frying involves cooking food in a hot pan with a small amount of oil, creating a direct contact between the heat source and the food.

2. Radiant Heat: Radiant heat refers to cooking methods where heat is emitted from a source without direct contact with the food. This includes baking, roasting, and toasting. In baking, the heat source is the oven, which produces radiant heat that circulates evenly around the food. This gentle and consistent heat is ideal for cooking delicate pastries, bread, and cakes. Roasting involves cooking food, often meat or vegetables, in the oven at a higher temperature to achieve browning and caramelization. Toasting utilizes radiant heat from a toaster or oven's broiler element to crisp and brown the surface of bread or other ingredients.

3. Conductive Heat: Conductive heat refers to cooking methods where heat is transferred through direct contact between the cooking vessel and the food. This includes methods such as sautéing, simmering, boiling, and steaming.

Sautéing involves cooking food quickly in a hot pan with a small amount of fat, utilizing conductive heat to achieve browning and flavorful crusts. Simmering involves cooking food in liquid over low heat, allowing the gentle transfer of heat and the development of rich flavors. Boiling refers to cooking food in a liquid at its boiling point, which is ideal for pasta, grains, and certain vegetables. Steaming involves cooking food above boiling water, utilizing the steam's heat to gently cook ingredients while preserving their natural flavors and nutrients.

4. Indirect Heat: Indirect heat is often used for slow and gentle cooking methods, such as braising and smoking. In braising, food is first seared or browned using direct heat, then cooked slowly in a covered pot with a small amount of liquid at a low temperature. This method allows for the tenderization of tougher cuts of meat and the development of rich, flavorful sauces. Smoking involves the use of indirect heat and smoke generated from burning wood chips or charcoal to cook food slowly over a longer period, infusing it with a distinct smoky flavor.

5. Hybrid Heat Sources: Modern kitchens often feature hybrid heat sources, such as convection ovens and induction cooktops. Convection ovens utilize a combination of radiant heat and a fan to circulate hot air, resulting in faster and more even cooking. Induction cooktops use magnetic fields to directly heat the cookware, providing precise control over the temperature and quick responsiveness.

Understanding the characteristics and techniques associated with different heat sources empowers cooks to select the most suitable method for each dish, ensuring optimal results. By harnessing the power of heat, chefs can transform ingredients, unlock flavors, and create culinary masterpieces that delight the senses.

Heat and Flavor Development

Heat is not only essential for cooking food but also plays a significant role in the development and transformation of flavors. Through the application of heat, flavors are intensified, ingredients undergo chemical reactions, and new tastes and aromas are created. Understanding how heat affects flavor development allows cooks to manipulate and enhance the taste profiles of their dishes, resulting in delicious and well-balanced culinary creations.

1. Maillard Reaction: One of the most crucial flavor-developing reactions that occur when heat is applied to food is the Maillard reaction. This chemical reaction takes place between amino acids and reducing sugars in the presence of heat, resulting in the browning and development of complex flavors and aromas. The Maillard reaction is responsible for the savory notes, nutty aromas, and rich flavors found in seared meats, roasted vegetables, and baked goods. By controlling the temperature and duration of heat exposure, cooks can achieve various degrees of Maillard reaction, from light browning to deep caramelization, adding depth and complexity to their dishes.

2. Caramelization: Caramelization is another flavor-enhancing process that occurs when sugar molecules are heated, breaking down and transforming into compounds that contribute to a sweet and rich taste. The application of heat causes the sugars to melt, darken, and release a distinctive caramel flavor. Caramelization is commonly observed when sautéing onions until they turn golden brown, roasting vegetables to bring out their natural sweetness, or creating caramel sauces and desserts. The depth and intensity of caramelization can be controlled by adjusting the heat and cooking time, allowing for the creation of different flavor profiles.

3. Reduction: Heat is often used to reduce the moisture content in sauces, stocks, and other liquids, leading to the concentration of flavors. When liquids are simmered or boiled, water evaporates, leaving behind a more concentrated mixture with intensified flavors. Reduction helps to enhance the richness, thickness, and complexity of sauces, allowing flavors to become more pronounced. This technique is commonly used in the preparation of reductions, gravies, and glazes.

4. Roasting and Grilling: The application of high heat in roasting and grilling not only cooks the food but also imparts distinctive flavors. Roasting involves cooking food in an oven at elevated temperatures, resulting in the caramelization of sugars, the Maillard reaction, and the development of deep, savory flavors. Grilling over an open flame or hot coals adds a unique smokiness and charred flavor to meats, vegetables, and even fruits, enhancing the overall taste experience.

5. Infusing Heat: Heat is also used to infuse flavors into ingredients and liquids. Techniques such as steeping, simmering, and frying allow ingredients like herbs, spices, and aromatics to release their flavors into oils, broths, and other mediums. This process of heat infusion helps to extract and meld the aromatic compounds, adding depth and complexity to the final dish.

6. Gentle Heat for Delicate Flavors: While high heat is often associated with flavor development, gentle heat is equally important for preserving delicate flavors. Lower temperatures can be used to maintain the freshness and subtlety of certain ingredients, such as herbs, delicate fruits, and fragile aromatics. By using low heat methods like steaming, poaching, or sous vide, cooks can preserve the delicate flavors and textures of these ingredients, ensuring they shine through in the final dish.

Understanding the relationship between heat and flavor development empowers cooks to utilize temperature control as a tool for creating dishes with complex and well-balanced taste profiles. By applying the appropriate level of heat and employing various cooking techniques, chefs can coax out the full potential of ingredients, transforming them into delectable culinary masterpieces that delight the senses.

Controlling Heat for Optimal Cooking Results

Mastering the art of controlling heat is essential for achieving optimal cooking results. Different dishes and ingredients require specific temperature ranges and techniques to ensure they are cooked to perfection. Understanding how to control heat allows cooks to maintain consistency, prevent overcooking or undercooking, and bring out the best flavors and textures in their culinary creations. Here are some key factors to consider when controlling heat in the kitchen:

1. Stovetop Heat Control: On a stovetop, heat control is primarily achieved through adjusting the burner settings or manipulating the flame intensity. Gas burners offer more immediate and precise heat control compared to electric cooktops. For gas burners, adjusting the flame size or position can regulate the heat. With electric burners, adjusting the temperature dial can control the heat output. Understanding the heat levels of each burner and how they correspond to different cooking techniques is essential for achieving desired results.

2. Oven Temperature Control: Oven temperature control is crucial for baking, roasting, and braising. Most ovens have temperature knobs or digital controls that allow cooks to set specific heat levels. It's important to preheat the oven to the desired temperature before placing food inside, as this ensures even cooking throughout. To ensure accurate oven temperatures, it's advisable to use an oven thermometer to verify the actual heat inside the oven, as oven thermostats may not always be completely accurate.

3. Heat Transfer Mediums: Understanding the heat transfer characteristics of different mediums is vital for controlling heat. For example, a thick-bottomed pan will retain and distribute heat more evenly than a thin pan. Cast iron pans have excellent heat retention properties, while stainless steel pans heat up quickly but may have uneven heat distribution. Non-stick pans heat up faster but require lower heat settings to prevent food from sticking. By selecting the appropriate cookware and adjusting the heat accordingly, cooks can optimize the cooking process.

4. Adjusting Heat Levels: Controlling heat levels during cooking is crucial for achieving desired outcomes. Higher heat settings are suitable for techniques like searing, stir-frying, and achieving caramelization. Lower heat settings are ideal for gentle simmering, slow cooking, and delicate ingredients. Adjusting the heat level can be done by increasing or decreasing burner settings, adjusting flame size, or moving the pan to a cooler or hotter part of the stovetop. This level of control ensures that food is cooked evenly and to the desired level of doneness.

5. Timing and Monitoring: Proper timing and monitoring are essential for controlling heat. Keeping track of cooking times helps prevent overcooking or undercooking. Use timers or alarms to remind you when to check the food. Regularly monitoring the cooking process, especially for techniques like sautéing or frying, allows for adjustments to heat levels as needed. Paying close attention to the color, texture, and aroma of the food can help determine if the heat needs to be increased, decreased, or maintained.

6. Resting and Carryover Cooking: Understanding the concept of resting and carryover cooking is crucial for achieving optimal results. Resting refers to allowing cooked food to sit off the heat for a few minutes before serving. This allows the internal temperature to stabilize, juices to redistribute, and flavors to intensify. Carryover cooking occurs when the residual heat continues to cook the food even after it has been removed from the heat source. Taking into account these factors helps prevent overcooking and ensures that the food is cooked to the desired level of doneness.

By mastering the control of heat in the kitchen, cooks can achieve consistent and delicious results. It's essential to familiarize oneself with the heat settings of different cooking appliances, understand the characteristics of heat transfer mediums, and make necessary adjustments based on the cooking technique and desired outcome. With practice and attention to detail, controlling heat becomes second nature, allowing for culinary mastery and the creation of truly exceptional dishes.

"Believe in the Magic of your Own Creativity and Let The Salt Fat Acid Heat Cookbook Empower you to Create Flavors that Mesmerize."

Chapter 11. Mastering Cooking Techniques with Heat

Grilling and Barbecuing: Achieving Smoky Perfection

Grilling and barbecuing are beloved cooking techniques that bring out incredible flavors, impart a tantalizing smokiness, and create a sense of outdoor cooking adventure. Whether you're grilling succulent steaks, charring vegetables, or slow-smoking ribs, mastering the art of grilling and barbecuing allows you to achieve smoky perfection and create memorable culinary experiences. Here are key aspects to consider when embracing these techniques:

1. Choosing the Right Grill: Selecting the appropriate grill is crucial for achieving optimal results. There are various options available, including charcoal grills, gas grills, pellet grills, and electric grills. Charcoal grills offer the classic smoky flavor and intense heat, while gas grills provide convenience and precise temperature control. Pellet grills combine the flavor of wood pellets with the ease of use, and electric grills are suitable for indoor grilling. Understanding the pros and cons of each type of grill allows you to choose the one that best suits your needs and desired cooking style.

2. Preparing the Grill: Properly preparing the grill sets the foundation for successful grilling or barbecuing. For charcoal grills, start by arranging charcoal briquettes or lump charcoal in a pyramid shape and add lighter fluid or use a chimney starter to ignite the coals. Allow the coals to ash over before spreading them out for direct or indirect heat cooking. Gas grills require preheating by turning on the burners and allowing the grill to heat up for several minutes. Preheating ensures even heat distribution and prevents food from sticking to the grates.

3. Direct and Indirect Heat: Understanding the concept of direct and indirect heat is essential for achieving desired cooking results. Direct heat is used for searing and cooking food quickly over high heat directly above the flame or burner. This method is suitable for thin cuts of meat or vegetables that cook relatively fast. Indirect heat involves placing the food away from the heat source and cooking it with the lid closed. This method is ideal for larger cuts of meat or delicate ingredients that require slower, more gentle cooking. Utilizing both direct and indirect heat allows for versatility and optimal flavor development.

4. Marinating and Seasoning: Marinating and seasoning your ingredients before grilling or barbecuing adds depth and complexity to the flavors. Marinades help tenderize and infuse flavors into meats, while dry rubs or spice blends create a flavorful crust on the exterior. Allow sufficient time for the flavors to penetrate the ingredients by marinating for a few hours or overnight in the refrigerator. Remember to remove excess marinade or pat dry the ingredients before grilling to prevent flare-ups.

5. Smoking Techniques: Smoking is a technique that adds an irresistible smoky flavor to grilled or barbecued food. Wood chips, chunks, or pellets can be used to create the smoke. Soaking wood chips in water for about 30 minutes before using them helps prolong the smoking process. For gas grills, you can use a smoker box or aluminum foil pouch filled with soaked wood chips placed directly on the burner to create smoke. Charcoal grills allow for the addition of wood chunks or chips directly to the coals. Experiment with different wood varieties like hickory, mesquite, applewood, or cherry to discover your favorite flavor profiles.

6. Temperature Control: Maintaining proper temperature control is crucial for achieving consistent results. For direct heat cooking, preheat the grill to high temperature (around 400-450°F/200-230°C) and adjust the burner or coal arrangement for varying heat zones. For indirect heat cooking, aim for a lower temperature (around 275-325°F/135-160°C) and use a drip pan to catch the fat drippings and prevent flare-ups. Monitoring the grill temperature using a built-in thermometer or a digital probe thermometer ensures precision and helps avoid overcooking or undercooking.

7. Timing and Grill Maintenance: Timing is key when grilling or barbecuing. Each ingredient and recipe will have specific cooking times, so it's important to follow guidelines or use a meat thermometer to check for doneness. Keep in mind that the cooking time can vary based on the heat intensity, the thickness of the ingredients, and personal preferences for doneness. Regularly turning and flipping the food promotes even cooking and prevents charring or burning. Additionally, proper grill maintenance, including cleaning the grates and removing ash or debris, ensures consistent heat distribution and extends the life of your grill.

8. Resting and Serving: Allowing grilled or barbecued food to rest after cooking is essential for redistributing the juices and ensuring tenderness. Cover the cooked meat loosely with foil and let it rest for a few minutes before serving. This resting period enhances the flavors and juiciness of the food. Serve the grilled or barbecued dishes with accompanying sauces, salsas, or side dishes that complement the smoky flavors and elevate the overall dining experience.

With these tips and techniques in mind, you can embark on a culinary adventure of grilling and barbecuing, creating delicious dishes infused with smoky perfection. Whether you're hosting a backyard barbecue or seeking the joy of outdoor cooking, embrace the art of grilling and delight in the enticing flavors and aromas that it brings.

Searing and Roasting: Building Rich Flavors

Searing and roasting are cooking techniques that create rich, complex flavors and textures in a wide range of ingredients. Whether you're searing a steak to achieve a caramelized crust or roasting vegetables to bring out their natural sweetness, mastering these techniques is key to unlocking delicious culinary creations. Here's a closer look at searing and roasting and how they contribute to building rich flavors:

1. Searing: Searing involves cooking ingredients at high heat to develop a flavorful crust on the surface. It is typically done with proteins like meat or fish but can also be applied to vegetables. The high heat triggers the Maillard reaction, a chemical reaction between amino acids and sugars that results in browning and the creation of complex, savory flavors. To achieve a successful sear, follow these steps:

- Start with a hot skillet or pan: Preheat the pan over medium-high to high heat until it is hot enough to produce a sizzling sound when you add the ingredients.

- Dry the ingredients: Pat the ingredients dry with paper towels before searing. Moisture on the surface can inhibit browning.
- Use oil with a high smoke point: Choose an oil like canola, vegetable, or grapeseed oil that can withstand high temperatures without smoking. Add enough oil to coat the bottom of the pan evenly.
- Don't overcrowd the pan: Leave enough space between the ingredients so that they can sear properly. Overcrowding can lead to steaming instead of searing.
- Resist the urge to flip or move the ingredients prematurely: Allow them to sear undisturbed for a few minutes on each side to develop a golden-brown crust. This step is crucial for flavor development.

2. Roasting: Roasting is a dry heat cooking method that involves cooking ingredients in the oven at a moderate to high temperature. It is particularly suited for meats, poultry, fish, and vegetables. Roasting allows ingredients to cook evenly, caramelize, and develop deep, concentrated flavors. Here are some key considerations for successful roasting:

- Preheat the oven: Ensure that the oven is preheated to the desired temperature before placing the ingredients inside. This helps with even cooking and consistent browning.
- Seasoning: Season the ingredients with salt, pepper, and other desired herbs and spices to enhance their flavors. You can also marinate or coat them with a flavorful rub before roasting.
- Use a roasting pan or baking sheet: Choose a pan with low sides or a rimmed baking sheet to allow for proper air circulation and even browning.
- Arrange ingredients in a single layer: Avoid overcrowding the pan, as this can lead to steaming rather than roasting. Leave enough space between the ingredients to allow for heat circulation.
- Monitor the cooking time: Cooking times will vary based on the size and thickness of the ingredients. Use a meat thermometer or visual cues to determine when the ingredients are cooked to the desired level of doneness.

- Basting and adding liquids: Basting ingredients with pan juices or adding flavorful liquids during the roasting process can enhance the richness and moisture of the final dish.
- Searing and roasting work well in combination too. For example, searing a piece of meat before roasting it in the oven helps develop a flavorful crust and seal in the juices. This technique is often used for roasts, poultry, and thick cuts of meat.

By mastering the art of searing and roasting, you can create dishes with deep, caramelized flavors, appealing textures, and irresistible aromas. These techniques add complexity and richness to your culinary repertoire, allowing you to elevate your cooking to new heights. Whether you're preparing a special meal for guests or indulging in a comforting family dinner, searing and roasting provide the foundation for building truly delicious and memorable flavors.

Simmering and Braising: Tender and Succulent Delights

Simmering and braising are cooking techniques that transform tough cuts of meat, poultry, and vegetables into tender, succulent delights. These methods utilize low, gentle heat over an extended period, allowing flavors to meld and ingredients to become fork-tender. Whether you're simmering a hearty stew or braising a pot roast, mastering these techniques will elevate your culinary skills and create satisfying, melt-in-your-mouth dishes. Let's explore the art of simmering and braising in more detail:

1. Simmering: Simmering is a cooking technique where ingredients are gently cooked in liquid at a temperature just below the boiling point. This slow and steady method extracts flavors from the ingredients while ensuring they remain tender. Simmering is commonly used for soups, stocks, sauces, and delicate proteins like fish. Here are some key considerations for successful simmering:

- Choose the right pot: Opt for a heavy-bottomed pot with a tight-fitting lid to distribute heat evenly and prevent excessive evaporation.

- Adjust heat: Start by bringing the liquid to a boil, then reduce the heat to maintain a gentle simmer. Bubbles should break the surface without vigorous boiling.
- Use flavorful liquids: Simmering allows ingredients to absorb the flavors of the liquid they are cooked in. Use broths, stocks, wine, or aromatic infusions to enhance the taste profile.
- Add ingredients progressively: Start with ingredients that require longer cooking times, such as root vegetables or tougher cuts of meat. Gradually add more delicate ingredients to prevent overcooking.
- Skim and strain: Remove any impurities or foam that rise to the surface during simmering to ensure a clear, clean-tasting liquid. Strain the liquid before serving if desired.
- Monitor cooking time: Different ingredients have varying cooking times. Regularly check for doneness and adjust the cooking time accordingly.

2. Braising: Braising involves first searing ingredients in fat, then slowly cooking them in a covered pot with a small amount of liquid. This method breaks down tough connective tissues, resulting in fork-tender meats and vegetables. Braising is perfect for tougher cuts of meat like chuck roast, short ribs, or lamb shanks. Follow these steps for successful braising:

- Sear for flavor: Start by browning the ingredients in hot oil or fat to develop a caramelized crust and enhance the flavor. This step adds depth and richness to the final dish.
- Choose the right pot: Use a heavy, oven-safe pot with a tight-fitting lid to ensure even heat distribution and retention.
- Add liquid and aromatics: Pour in enough liquid (such as broth, wine, or a combination) to partially submerge the ingredients. Add aromatics like onions, garlic, herbs, and spices to infuse flavors.
- Cover and transfer to the oven: Cover the pot with the lid and transfer it to a preheated oven. The low, gentle heat of the oven ensures even cooking and allows the flavors to meld together.
- Baste and check for doneness: Occasionally baste the ingredients with the cooking liquid to keep them

moist. Check for doneness by testing the tenderness with a fork. Adjust the cooking time as needed.

- Reduce and thicken the sauce: Once the ingredients are tender, remove them from the pot and set aside. Skim off any excess fat and reduce the cooking liquid on the stovetop to concentrate flavors and create a luscious sauce.

Simmering and braising offer a world of possibilities for creating tender and succulent dishes. These techniques coax out the natural flavors of the ingredients and transform them into comforting, mouthwatering delights. Whether you're preparing a hearty stew, a flavorful braise, or a delicate fish dish, mastering simmering and braising will bring you closer to culinary excellence and elevate your dining experiences.

"Embrace the Beauty of Imperfection and let the Symphony of Salt, Fat, Acid and Heat Guide you Towards Culinary Excellence."

Chapter 12. Heat Around the Globe: Techniques and Inspirations

Spicy Heat in Indian and Thai Cuisines

Indian and Thai cuisines are renowned for their vibrant flavors, and a key component that sets them apart is the delightful heat derived from spicy ingredients. Both cuisines expertly utilize a wide array of spices, chilies, and aromatic herbs to create dishes that are bold, complex, and exhilarating to the palate. Let's delve into the world of spicy heat in Indian and Thai cuisines:

1. Spices and Chilies in Indian Cuisine: Indian cuisine is a tapestry of flavors, and spices play a central role in creating its distinctive taste. Spices like cumin, coriander, turmeric, cardamom, cinnamon, and cloves infuse dishes with depth, warmth, and complexity. Alongside these spices, chilies are essential for adding heat to Indian recipes. Varieties of chilies such as green chilies, red chilies, and dried chili powders are commonly used. Here are some key points to note:

- Heat levels: Indian cuisine offers a range of heat levels, from mildly spiced dishes to fiery hot curries. The heat can be adjusted based on personal preference or the region the recipe originates from.
- Spice blends: Indian cuisine is renowned for its spice blends, such as garam masala, curry powder, and tikka masala. These blends often include chili powder or crushed chilies, adding both heat and flavor complexity.
- Regional variations: Different regions of India have their own spice preferences and chili varieties. For example, the southern states of India often use more dried red chilies, while the northeastern regions incorporate unique local chilies.
- Balancing heat: In Indian cooking, the heat from chilies is balanced with other ingredients like yogurt, coconut milk, tomatoes, or lime juice. This balance helps to enhance the overall flavor profile of the dish.

2. Chilies and Aromatic Herbs in Thai Cuisine: Thai cuisine is renowned for its harmonious blend of flavors, which often includes a fiery kick of heat. Chilies and aromatic herbs are key ingredients used to achieve this balance of flavors. Thai cuisine features a variety of chilies, including bird's eye chilies, Thai chili peppers, and dried chili flakes. Here's what you should know:

- Heat levels: Thai cuisine showcases a spectrum of heat levels, ranging from mild to extremely spicy. Some dishes, such as the famous green or red curry, are known for their intense spiciness, while others offer a milder heat profile.
- Aromatic herbs: Thai cuisine incorporates aromatic herbs like lemongrass, galangal, kaffir lime leaves, and Thai basil. These herbs complement the heat of chilies and add layers of fragrance and complexity to the dishes.
- Balance of flavors: Thai cuisine emphasizes a balance of flavors known as "hot, sour, sweet, and salty." The heat from chilies is counterbalanced with sour ingredients like lime juice, sweetness from palm sugar, and saltiness from fish sauce or soy sauce.

- Condiments and sauces: Thai cuisine offers a range of spicy condiments and sauces, such as nam prik, sriracha, and chili pastes. These add an extra kick of heat to dishes and allow diners to customize their desired spice level.

The inclusion of spicy heat in Indian and Thai cuisines adds depth, intensity, and excitement to the dining experience. Whether it's the aromatic blend of spices in an Indian curry or the fiery heat of a Thai stir-fry, these cuisines offer a journey of flavors that ignite the senses and leave a lasting impression.

Fiery Flavors in Mexican and Caribbean Cooking

Fiery Flavors in Mexican and Caribbean Cooking

Mexican and Caribbean cuisines are known for their vibrant and bold flavors, and a significant element that contributes to their distinctive taste profiles is the fiery heat derived from various chili peppers and spices. These cuisines expertly incorporate a wide range of peppers, such as jalapenos, habaneros, Scotch bonnets, and serranos, to create dishes that are both spicy and delicious. Let's explore the fiery flavors of Mexican and Caribbean cooking:

1. Chili Peppers in Mexican Cuisine: Mexican cuisine is renowned for its use of chili peppers, which add depth, complexity, and a fiery kick to dishes. Here are some key points about the use of chili peppers in Mexican cooking:

- Variety of chili peppers: Mexico boasts a rich diversity of chili peppers, each with its own unique flavor profile and heat level. From the mild and versatile poblano pepper to the intensely spicy habanero, there is a chili pepper for every palate.
- Commonly used peppers: Some commonly used chili peppers in Mexican cuisine include jalapeno, serrano, guajillo, ancho, and chipotle. These peppers range in heat levels and are used in various forms, such as fresh, dried, or smoked.
- Spice blends and sauces: Mexican cuisine features spice blends like chili powder, which combines dried chili peppers with other spices like cumin, garlic, and oregano. Additionally, fiery sauces like salsa roja,

salsa verde, and hot sauces made with habanero or chipotle peppers are popular accompaniments.

- Balancing flavors: In Mexican cuisine, the heat from chili peppers is balanced with other ingredients like tomatoes, onions, garlic, cilantro, lime juice, and Mexican cheeses. This balance of flavors adds complexity and harmony to the dishes.

2. Spices and Peppers in Caribbean Cuisine: Caribbean cuisine is known for its vibrant and spicy flavors, showcasing the influence of various cultures and the use of local ingredients. Here's what you need to know about the fiery flavors in Caribbean cooking:

- Scotch bonnet and habanero peppers: These peppers are widely used in Caribbean cuisine and are known for their fiery heat. They provide a distinct and intense spiciness that is a hallmark of Caribbean dishes.
- Jerk seasoning: One of the most famous spice blends in Caribbean cuisine is jerk seasoning. It combines ingredients like allspice, thyme, ginger, scallions, garlic, and fiery Scotch bonnet peppers. This blend is

often used to marinate and season meats, infusing them with a fiery and aromatic flavor.

- Pepper sauces: Caribbean cuisine offers a variety of pepper sauces that range in heat level, from mildly spicy to scorching hot. These sauces are made with a combination of chili peppers, vinegar, citrus juices, and spices. They are used as condiments to add an extra kick to dishes.
- Spice rubs and marinades: Caribbean cuisine incorporates spice rubs and marinades that feature a blend of spices, herbs, and fiery peppers. These are applied to meats, seafood, or vegetables, infusing them with intense flavors and heat.
- Local ingredients: Caribbean cuisine utilizes an abundance of fresh and flavorful ingredients like tropical fruits, coconut, citrus, and herbs like thyme and cilantro. These ingredients complement the spicy heat and provide a balance of flavors.

The fiery flavors of Mexican and Caribbean cooking bring a thrilling intensity to the palate. Whether it's the smoky depth of Mexican chipotle or the scorching heat of Caribbean Scotch bonnet, these cuisines celebrate the power of chili peppers and spices, creating unforgettable culinary experiences that awaken the senses.

Exploring Heat in African and Middle Eastern Dishes

African and Middle Eastern cuisines are known for their bold and flavorful dishes that often incorporate a delightful level of heat. Spices, peppers, and aromatic herbs are expertly used to add complexity, depth, and a fiery kick to the culinary creations of these regions. Let's dive into the world of heat in African and Middle Eastern dishes:

1. Spice Blends and Peppers in African Cuisine: African cuisine is incredibly diverse, with each region showcasing its unique flavors and spice profiles. Here are some key aspects of heat in African cooking:

- Berbere and Harissa: In Ethiopian and North African cuisines, respectively, spice blends like berbere and harissa feature prominently. These blends often contain chili peppers, along with a mix of spices such as cumin, coriander, paprika, fenugreek, and garlic.

They lend a rich, fiery flavor to stews, sauces, and grilled meats.

- Scotch bonnet and Bird's Eye Chilies: These chilies are commonly used in West African cuisine, bringing both heat and distinct flavor to dishes. They are utilized in a variety of forms, including fresh, dried, and ground, and can be found in soups, stews, and marinades.
- Peri-Peri Sauce: Originating from Southern Africa, peri-peri sauce is made from African bird's eye chilies (also known as peri-peri chilies), combined with citrus juices, garlic, herbs, and spices. This sauce adds a fiery punch to grilled meats, seafood, and even vegetables.
- Xawaash: Found in Somali cuisine, xawaash is a spice blend that typically includes coriander, cumin, cardamom, cinnamon, cloves, and chili powder. It adds a warm and subtly spicy flavor to dishes like stews, rice, and meat preparations.

2. Spices and Peppers in Middle Eastern Cuisine: Middle Eastern cuisine is renowned for its aromatic spices and a well-balanced use of heat. Here's what you need to know about exploring heat in Middle Eastern dishes:

- Aleppo Pepper: Named after the Syrian city of Aleppo, this pepper delivers a moderate heat level with fruity and slightly smoky undertones. It is used in various Middle Eastern dishes, including kebabs, roasted vegetables, and soups.
- Sumac: While not inherently spicy, sumac is a tangy spice commonly used in Middle Eastern cuisine. Its tartness adds depth and brightness to dishes, enhancing the overall flavor profile and complementing other spices and ingredients.
- Baharat: This spice blend is popular in Middle Eastern cuisine and typically includes black pepper, cinnamon, cardamom, cloves, cumin, coriander, and nutmeg. It adds a warm and aromatic heat to dishes like grilled meats, stews, and rice preparations.
- Zesty Herb Pastes: Middle Eastern cuisine utilizes herb pastes, such as zhug and charmoula, which combine fresh herbs like cilantro, parsley, mint, with garlic, lemon juice, and chili peppers. These pastes infuse dishes with vibrant flavors and a pleasant heat.

- Dried Red Chilies: Various dried red chili peppers, such as Aleppo, Turkish, or Moroccan chilies, are used in Middle Eastern cuisine to add heat and depth of flavor to sauces, stews, and spice rubs.

The use of heat in African and Middle Eastern dishes adds an exciting dimension to the culinary experience. Whether it's the complex spice blends of Ethiopian cuisine or the aromatic herbs and peppers in Middle Eastern cuisine, these regions celebrate the art of balancing heat with other flavors, creating memorable and delicious dishes that truly captivate the taste buds.

"Turn Ordinary Meals to Extraordinary Experiences as you Harness the Power of Salt, Fat, Acid and Heat with The Salt Fat Acid Heat Cookbook."

Conclusion

Congratulations! You have embarked on a culinary journey that has taken you through the powerful elements of salt, fat, acid, and heat. You have discovered how these fundamental components can transform ordinary dishes into extraordinary culinary creations. By understanding their roles and mastering their application, you have unlocked the key to culinary mastery and unleashed your creativity in the kitchen.

Throughout this cookbook, we have explored the intricacies of each element, delving into their flavors, techniques, and cultural influences. We have learned how salt enhances and balances flavors, how fat brings richness and texture, how acidity brightens and harmonizes, and how heat develops and transforms ingredients. With this knowledge, you are now equipped to elevate your cooking to new heights.

Remember, cooking is an art, and you are the artist. Just as a painter selects colors and brushes to create a masterpiece, you can now choose the perfect combination of salt, fat, acid, and heat to bring your culinary creations to life. Whether you are crafting a delicate sauce, searing a tender cut of meat, or infusing your dishes with exotic flavors, you have the tools to create irresistible flavors and culinary marvels.

But this journey is not just about technique and skill. It is about passion and creativity. It is about embracing the joy and excitement of experimenting with different ingredients, flavors, and cuisines. It is about infusing your dishes with your unique personality and adding that extra touch of magic to every bite. It is about the joy of sharing your creations with loved ones and witnessing the delight on their faces as they savor the flavors you have carefully crafted.

So, go forth with confidence and embrace the power of salt, fat, acid, and heat. Let your imagination run wild and explore new culinary horizons. Experiment with flavors, techniques, and cultural influences from around the world. Trust your instincts, but also be open to learning and growing as a cook.

Remember, culinary mastery is a lifelong journey. It requires practice, patience, and a hunger for knowledge. As you continue to refine your skills and expand your culinary repertoire, always stay curious and never be afraid to push the boundaries of your creativity.

With this cookbook as your guide, you now possess the knowledge and inspiration to create irresistible flavors and unforgettable dining experiences. So, step into your kitchen, gather your ingredients, and let your culinary adventure begin. Embrace the power of salt, fat, acid, and heat, and let your culinary mastery shine through in every dish you create.

Bon appétit!

Appendix A: Glossary of Culinary Terms

Acidulate: To add acid, such as lemon juice or vinegar, to a dish to enhance its flavor or preserve ingredients.

Braise: A cooking method that involves searing food in fat, then cooking it slowly in a covered pot with a small amount of liquid, resulting in tender and flavorful dishes.

Brining: The process of soaking food, usually meat or poultry, in a solution of water, salt, and sometimes sugar and spices, to enhance its flavor, juiciness, and tenderness.

Caramelization: The process of heating sugars, either in their natural form or added to food, until they turn golden brown, creating a rich and complex flavor.

Deglaze: To add liquid, such as wine or broth, to a pan in which food has been cooked, scraping the browned bits from the bottom, to create a flavorful sauce or base for a dish.

Emulsify: To combine two liquids, such as oil and vinegar, that do not naturally mix together by slowly adding one to the other while whisking vigorously to create a stable mixture.

Infuse: To steep ingredients, such as herbs, spices, or fruits, in a liquid, such as water or oil, to extract their flavors and aromas.

Mise en place: A French term that means "everything in its place," referring to the practice of prepping and organizing ingredients and tools before starting to cook.

Poach: To cook food gently in a liquid, typically water or broth, at a low temperature, ensuring tenderness and retaining moisture.

Roux: A mixture of equal parts fat, such as butter or oil, and flour, used as a thickening agent for sauces, soups, and stews.

Sear: To cook food quickly over high heat to brown its surface, sealing in juices and adding flavor.

Simmer: To cook food in a liquid at a temperature just below boiling, maintaining gentle bubbles and a steady heat.

Toast: To brown food, such as bread or nuts, by exposing it to dry heat, enhancing its flavor and creating a crisp texture.

Whip: To beat ingredients vigorously, usually with a whisk or electric mixer, to incorporate air and increase volume, resulting in a light and fluffy texture.

Appendix B: Measurement Conversions

Cooking is a precise art that often requires accurate measurements to achieve the desired results. As you delve into the world of culinary mastery, it is essential to have a handy reference for converting measurements. This appendix provides a comprehensive guide to help you convert common cooking measurements, ensuring that your recipes turn out perfectly every time.

1. Volume Conversions:

- 1 teaspoon (tsp) = 5 milliliters (ml)
- 1 tablespoon (tbsp) = 15 milliliters (ml)
- 1 fluid ounce (fl oz) = 30 milliliters (ml)
- 1 cup = 240 milliliters (ml)
- 1 pint (pt) = 480 milliliters (ml)
- 1 quart (qt) = 960 milliliters (ml)
- 1 liter (L) = 1,000 milliliters (ml)
- 1 gallon (gal) = 3,785 milliliters (ml)

2. Weight Conversions:

- 1 ounce (oz) = 28 grams (g)
- 1 pound (lb) = 16 ounces (oz) = 454 grams (g)
- 1 kilogram (kg) = 1,000 grams (g) = 2.2 pounds (lbs)
- 3. Temperature Conversions:
- Celsius (°C) to Fahrenheit (°F): Multiply the Celsius temperature by 9/5 and add 32.
- Fahrenheit (°F) to Celsius (°C): Subtract 32 from the Fahrenheit temperature and multiply by 5/9.

4. Cup Conversions:

- 1 cup = 16 tablespoons (tbsp)
- 1 cup = 48 teaspoons (tsp)
- 1 cup = 8 fluid ounces (fl oz)

5. Common Ingredient Conversions:

- Butter: 1 stick of butter = 1/2 cup = 8 tablespoons (tbsp) = 4 ounces (oz)
- Sugar: 1 cup of sugar = 200 grams (g)
- Flour: 1 cup of flour = 120 grams (g)
- Honey or Maple Syrup: 1 cup = 340 grams (g)

It is important to note that these conversions are approximate, and slight variations may occur depending on the specific ingredient and its density. Always refer to a trusted measurement conversion chart or use a digital scale for precise measurements when accuracy is crucial.

By having this measurement conversion guide at your fingertips, you can confidently navigate through recipes from different sources and adapt them to suit your needs. Whether you are scaling up a recipe to feed a larger crowd or making adjustments based on the ingredients you have on hand, these conversions will be your invaluable tool in the kitchen.

Remember, precision in measurements can make a significant difference in the outcome of your dishes. So, use this conversion guide as your trusty companion, and let it empower you to explore new recipes, experiment with flavors, and continue on your culinary journey with confidence.

Happy cooking and may your culinary creations always be a delightful success!

Made in the USA
Monee, IL
03 June 2023

35195996R00095